The Oak Park Strategy

Studies of Urban Society
Morris Janowitz, Gerald Suttles,
Richard Taub, series editors

Other books in this series:
Elijah Anderson, *A Place on the
 Corner*
Michael Crozier, *The World of the
 Office Worker*
Albert Hunter, *Symbolic
 Communities*
William Kornblum, *Blue Collar
 Community*
Robert McKenzie and Allan Silver,
 Angels in Marble
David Popenoe, *The Suburban
 Environment*
Gerald D. Suttles, *The Social Con-
 struction of Communities*
Gerald D. Suttles, *The Social Order
 of the Slum*
Mayer N. Zald, *Organizational
 Change*

Carole Goodwin

The Oak Park
Strategy

Community Control of Racial Change

The University of
Chicago Press
Chicago and London

The University of Chicago Press,
Chicago 60637
The University of Chicago Press, Ltd.,
London

Library of Congress Cataloging in Publication Data

Goodwin, Carole
  The Oak Park strategy.

  (Studies of urban society)
  Includes index.
  1. Oak Park, Ill.—Social conditions.
2. Oak Park, Ill.—Race relations.   3. Austin,
Ill.—Social conditions.   4. Austin, Ill.—Race
relations.   I. Title.
HN80.016G66   301.36′4′0977311   79–13651
ISBN 0–226–30396–9

Photographs by Ted Lacey.

CAROLE GOODWIN, former assistant
professor of sociology at Illinois Institute
of Technology, is a book dealer in Oak
Park.

For my parents

Contents

Illustrations

ix

Tables

Acknowledgments

I am indebted to many people for their assistance over the years this book has been in preparation. First of all, it probably would not have been completed without Morris Janowitz's continuing advice and encouragement, and his contributions to community theory are are fundamental to this work. The University of Chicago Center for Urban Studies provided me with a graduate fellowship and access to data essential to the research. Among those at the center who helped, Katherine Smith and Brian J. L. Berry deserve particular thanks. Carol Zientek helped in so many ways that her contribution cannot be adequately acknowledged, but I am grateful. Of course, the greatest thanks must go to the leaders and residents of Austin and Oak Park.

1

Introduction   Oak Park, Illinois, is a long-established middle-class community of more than 60,000 residents situated at Chicago's city limits, about nine miles west of Chicago's Loop. Until the very early 1970s, Oak Park, like the great majority of Chicago's suburbs at the time, was virtually all white, with only 132 black inhabitants on the 1970 census rolls.

East of Oak Park—just across Austin Boulevard, the boundary between Chicago and Oak Park—is the Chicago neighborhood of Austin. Throughout most of the 1960s, Austin was also middle-class and mostly white. But by 1970 much of Austin had undergone racial transition, as the western arm of Chicago's large black community extended itself, and by 1971 Oak Park also began to experience substantial black in-migration.

Yet six years later, while racial transition and resegregation of neighborhoods from white to black shifted northward in Austin, Oak Park had no resegregated black area, had a black population of less than 10 percent, had both blacks and whites moving into all of its geographical sectors, and was being touted in the local and national press as a case of successful neighborhood racial

integration. At least superficially, racial change in Austin conformed to a pattern set decades earlier in Chicago; but for the
events in Oak Park there was little if any precedent.

The research on which this book is based—a participant-
observation study of the Austin and Oak Park community responses to racial change—began before Oak Park had experienced much black in-migration. Oak Park's status as a white
suburb abutting a central-city ghetto offered an interesting opportunity to see whether racial change in such a context would
take the same form in the suburb as in the city. To this end, we
determined to compare the processes of change and community
responses to it in Austin and in Oak Park, particularly picking
out those elements that seemed closely if not inherently linked
to the urban and suburban characters of the two communities.
Of course the study in no way provides a definitive answer to
the general question of urban-suburban differences in racial
change, but it yields important descriptive data that suggest
and can help to ground eventual theoretical formulations.
Moreover, when a case fails to fulfill expectations based on
existing theory, it may indicate a need to rethink and perhaps
reformulate that theory.

Thus, through the fortunate timing of this study, we were
able to observe from a very early stage the emergence in Oak
Park of organization that thoroughly transformed the expected
course of racial change in that community. To wholly appreciate
the unexpectedness of the outcome in Oak Park, we must set
the case in its proper historical and theoretical context.

Invasion and Succession: Theory and History

The transition of residential communities from white to black
has been one of the most striking of urban processes over the
last few decades. Few urban phenomena have aroused as much
concern or spurred as much local reaction. For black people,
neighborhood transition has represented a gain in housing

supply, but one limited by the persisting barriers of segregation. The sharp demarcation of white and black residential areas and the shrinking of the former in the face of steady expansion of the latter has been one of the most important determinants of the housing choices and related behavior of inhabitants of the large cities of the United States regardless of race.

Years of racial discrimination have meant that the urban housing available to black people has been mainly in segregated black neighborhoods or in the blocks immediately adjacent to them. The latter, of course, are defined as "changing" and hence simultaneously become "undesirable" for whites, and the neighborhood soon resegregates. Once all white, the neighborhood becomes all black after a more or less brief period of biracial occupancy.

The best model of this process was developed in the 1920s by Ernest W. Burgess, professor of sociology at the University of Chicago, where he and his colleagues were inventing a mode of understanding urban communities known as human ecology, borrowing and modifying concepts used by biologists studying plants and animal communities. Thus Burgess gave the name "invasion and succession" to the cycle through which the character and composition of urban land areas was transformed as the city grew.

As Burgess originally described it, invasion-succession had four stages, not clearly demarcated, but overlapping and blending into one another. These were: (1) penetration, or first entry of newcomers or new land uses; (2) reaction to penetration by existing inhabitants; (3) continued influx of newcomers and abandonment of the area by its original inhabitants; and (4) climax, or complete displacement of the original inhabitants or land uses by the new ones.[1]

As an analysis of urban racial change (just one of its specific applications) the Burgess model has endured very well. In 1975 Aldrich undertook a comprehensive review of the scholarly writings on racial change and concluded that, with few exceptions, the invasion-succession model still provided an adequate explanation.[2]

Earlier, Otis D. Duncan and Beverly Duncan had used the model to guide their ambitious study of racial turnover in Chicago census tracts between 1940 and 1950.[3] The Duncans rearticulated the Burgess model to apply specifically to racial change, but their modifications were not substantial alterations of the model. They did identify a new phase of the process that they termed "piling-up"—that is, increasing density of residence throughout the entire process of transition. More significant for our purpose, Burgess's "reaction" stage was absent from the modified Duncan model. The method the Duncans used was not really capable of discerning the reactions of the original inhabitants of a census tract. But they found that once the invasion process had begun it was seldom reversed. Almost inevitably, total succession followed invasion, and, by implication, the reactions we may assume occurred were ineffective in altering the course of this process.

During the 1960s the front of ghetto expansion in Chicago traveled westward at a rate of about two blocks per year, and the total black residential concentration in the city enlarged at an average rate of three city blocks per week.[4] The projected path of its western arm would take it through the southern halves of both Austin and Oak Park. Historically, the pattern had been set: once the first stage of invasion began, the outcome was usually predictable. As we shall see, the experience of Austin fulfilled that prediction, whereas racial change in Oak Park broke from the expected form. A major task of this book is to explain Oak Park's departure from that pattern.

We often hear words such as "wave" or "rolling tide" used to describe the cumulative pattern of invasion and succession in cities. Examining cases like Austin leaves little surprise that such metaphors come so easily. Austin's experience, which I shall describe in following chapters, closely approximated the model of invasion-succession as a "natural" process. We may therefore be tempted to overlook the combination of interests, motives, and very concrete acts by individuals and groups that constitute neighborhood racial transition.

But when we confront cases like Oak Park, which seem to depart from expectations founded on the ecological model of

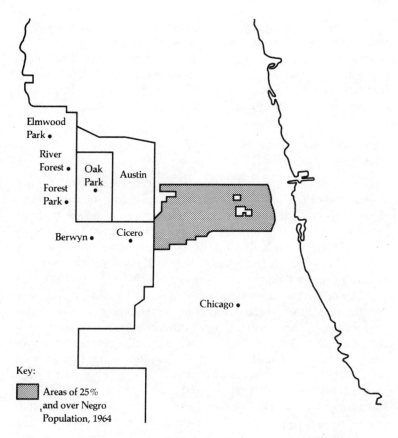

Fig. 1.   Austin and Oak Park in relation to nearby communities and to the black residential area on Chicago's west side. Source: Chicago Urban League, *Areas of Negro Residence, 1960, 1964* (Chicago: Chicago Urban League, 1965).

invasion-succession, we immediately realize the model's shortcomings and the need to analyze the situation in finer detail. In particular, we need to examine the socially organized behaviors and institutional patterns that have made total transition the nearly inevitable outcome of racial invasions and to explain why these forces were not similarly potent in Oak Park.

And, without doubting the general usefulness of ecological explanations, we must also ask to what extent people can take planned, purposeful, organized, and effective action to intervene in the course of such large-scale ecological processes as racial transition. This is the real importance, practically and theoretically, of studying Oak Park.

Related Theory and Research

As we have seen, the notion that ecological processes mirror the dynamics of urban change forms the backdrop of this study. Our research is also conceptually indebted to a second body of theory and research, represented by the literature that attempts to illuminate actual individual and group behavior in situations of racial change. In fact, it is to that analytical stream that this study properly belongs.

Eleanor Wolf applied the concept of the self-fulfilling prophecy to the study of racial transition, considering it the social psychological determinant of neighborhood turnover and some of its perceived concomitants such as decline in property values.[5] Although it has been usefully pointed out that prophecies of racial change are not always self-fulfilling,[6] the model does seem to represent adequately what occurs when neighborhoods do change. We need to know more about the conditions that give rise to such prophecies and about the situations when they are or are not self-fulfilling. If we accept Wolf's model, this is tantamount to discovering the conditions for neighborhood racial change.

Wolf's formulation seems to be a special restatement of W. I. Thomas's famous dictum regarding the definition of the situation: that what is perceived as real is real in its consequences. In this study, we shall see that the way local residents and institutional representatives define the situation is indeed of utmost importance for the outcome of the process of racial change.

The notion of the self-fulfilling prophecy simply illuminates one aspect of a complex phenomenon. Other theoretical statements have stressed other factors, such as white people's strong desire for cultural hegemony in their residential environments[7] or the degree of status threat racial change poses to members of different social classes.[8]

Case studies can be especially useful in bringing to light the behaviors and conditions underlying neighborhood change. Many such studies exist, ranging from analyses of single black families moving into white neighborhoods to examinations of entire communities undergoing change.[9] Among the best of the latter is Molotch's study of the South Shore neighborhood of Chicago.[10] Molotch focuses more on institutional than individual social psychological mechanisms as the important determinants of racial transition. In particular, he demonstrates how the segmentation of the housing market into two segregated components, yielding separate housing markets for blacks and whites, underlies the whole process of change and almost assures total transition in neighborhoods near the ghetto once they begin to experience black in-migration. The operation and the effects of this dual housing market are also important concerns of this research.

Another body of social scientific thought that is directly relevant is concerned not so much with the dynamics of racial change per se as with the more general nature and dynamics of community. The broad theme of this book is the community under change. The actual replacement of white residents by black residents is only one aspect of that change. As the white community anticipates or reacts to transition, processes are set in motion that affect the way residents perceive, define, and subjectively experience the community. The local community is altered as much by its attempts to ward off racial transition as by the transition itself. Thus we must look beyond studies of racial change to more general conceptualizations of neighborhood structure and dynamics.

For our purpose, the most useful of these is Morris Janowitz's concept of the "community of limited liability."[11] This idea emphasizes the voluntary, partial, and specialized nature of the individual's attachment to the local urban residential area. It assumes that individuals have variable but limited investments in their communities, investments that they may withdraw if the communities cease to meet their needs and expectations. While withdrawal need not mean physical departure, the flight of white residents from racially changing neighborhoods is a good example of the concept.

The community of limited liability model also gives attention to the role of local elites in representing the community; they act in its behalf, lend it its sense of integrity, and define its identity. We are dealing with large communities, not held together by primary ties and face-to-face interactions among ordinary residents. Their cohesion depends upon the networks of institutions, organizations, and leaders that form their local elites and are pivotal in maintaining the community as a perceived entity and in responding to the "threat" of racial change.

The community of limited liability is not a static, categorical concept. It implies a process of creating and defining the community that Suttles has referred to as the community's "social construction."[12] The construction of community is always a dynamic and ongoing process. But the perception of racial change is such that assumptions are undermined and definitions rendered inoperable in an unusually short time, necessitating a radical reconstruction of community. The process of transition and the community response to that process are dialectically related. As actual or prospective black in-migration and the community response to that stimulus interact, the fabric of community is continually rewoven. Change, the perception of change, the total definition of the situation, and strategies for coping or intervening all interact mutually and continuously. The nature of this interaction and its consequences in two particular communities, Austin and Oak Park, is the subject of this study.

Racial transition is conceived as an ecological process; the construction of communities, as a normative process. The two perspectives intersect in the perceptions and behaviors of individual residents and community leaders. The crucial issue, again, is whether people can voluntarily shape their own local environments or whether they must always be overwhelmed by larger institutional patterns and ecological forces. In most cases that have been described, the latter proposition has held. It is Oak Park's departure from this norm—a departure it effected without using its local powers to exclude blacks, as suburbs have often been alleged to do—that makes this community of special interest to both theorists and practitioners.

Method

The original motivation for this research was the general question whether neighborhood racial change stemming from an expanding urban ghetto would take the same form in the suburbs as it had in the city. Oak Park afforded one of the first opportunities in the Chicago area to begin to answer that question. From the beginning we concentrated particularly on the way the community responded to its perception of imminent racial change and observed the evolution of organization to cope with or combat racial change. Such organization had developed in practically all Chicago neighborhoods facing racial transition, usually to no avail. Though we did not know at the outset whether Oak Park's experience would be any different, it seemed valuable to study in close detail the process of community response as it developed, to be on the scene as it was evolving, and to compare the evolution of that response with the reaction to change in a city neighborhood.

We chose Austin as a counterpoint to Oak Park largely because of the geographic proximity of the two communities. There were, as we shall see, social and demographic differences between them, differences that were neither extreme nor, on the other hand, inconsequential. However, situated so closely together, Oak Park and Austin were subject to some of the same ecological forces at very nearly the same time. Although the communities differed in some respects, many of the conditions affecting them were the same. They were part of the same geographic subsector of the metropolitan housing market. And it was the same black residential area that residents of both Austin and Oak Park apprehensively saw advancing. Most important, the residents of Austin and Oak Park defined their situations as identical in many ways. They saw themselves as confronted with the same set of problems, and they expected to be directly and profoundly affected by events in the neighboring community. In short, they saw themselves as sharing the same plight.

Our approach used several methods, relying primarily on participant observation and related field methods such as unstructured interviews, use of informants, and thorough exploitation of documentary, archival, and media sources. Description is based on quantitative data from a variety of sources.

I lived in Austin from 1967 through 1971. Most of the field data on Austin were gathered through participant observation, most extensively between 1969 and 1971. The observation was most intensively concentrated in the central part of Austin that will be designated the "Town Hall area." To offset these temporal and geographic limitations, the data were augmented and updated by follow-up contacts and interviews in Austin and by media and documentary materials. Data were also drawn from a field report on Austin prepared at the University of Chicago's Center for Urban Studies.[13]

The most intensive observation in Oak Park, where I have lived since 1971, was done from January 1972 through August 1973. In both communities I undertook limited volunteer work in the major community organizations. I refrained, however, from becoming directly involved with two of Austin's most important organizations, the Organization for a Better Austin and the Town Hall Assembly. Because of the intense hostilities between the two, affiliation with either one would have jeopardized the research. I attended their meetings and interviewed their leaders, as I did for numerous other local organizations. The networks of overlapping memberships and affiliations brought me into contact with most of the organizational activists in both communities, even though I could hardly take an active part in all the groups. My descriptions and analyses of the residents' and nonresidents' perceptions of the communities and the process of change are products of many conversations and interviews with friends, neighbors, acquaintances, and strangers. While these do not constitute a systematically designed sample, they cover the spectra of age, race, sex, social class, and so forth, represented in the communities.

From 1974 on I continued to observe the activities of local organizations and government in Oak Park, but primarily as a resident and citizen, without the degree of organizational participation and involvement I had maintained during the actual study. As a resident, of course, I was still a participant in day-to-day neighborhood and community routine. By checking with informants active in voluntary organizations and government, by keeping abreast of local newspaper accounts of events, and by continuing to collect and peruse the reports and documents of governmental and voluntary agencies and organizations, I have been able to bring the account of Oak Park's ongoing integration efforts and results up to date through the end of 1977, although the description of events after 1974 lacks the depth afforded by intensive participant observation.

Oak Park was investigated in greater depth than Austin, and more attention is given to its description and interpretation. It was Oak Park, after all, that provided the heretofore relatively unstudied suburban dimension and that empirically departed from the typical pattern of block-to-block transition. It thus seemed of more interest to explain why Oak Park varied from this pattern than why Austin did not.

Given the initial rationale for the study, it was tempting to leap to the conclusion that Oak Park was different because it was a suburb. But, since there were other differences between Austin and Oak Park, we constantly had to assess their explanatory power apart from the city-suburb distinction. If we were to conclude that this distinction contributed to the explanation, we would have to demonstrate the connection logically or empirically. And this is what we have attempted to do. Although I will not argue that demographic and socioeconomic differences between the two communities were of no importance, the research suggests that suburban imagery, civic culture, and, especially, political organization strongly affected the conduct and outcome of Oak Park's strategy to control racial change.

This issue is of some theoretical importance, since urbanists, particularly those who take the human ecological perspective, commonly hold that the political divisions separating metropolitan municipalities are unrelated to ecological structure and thus do not affect large-scale ecological processes, of which racial transition is a prime case. The idea that there is a special, indigenous suburban character different from the city by its very suburban nature was a popular view in the 1950s. This "suburban myth" having been properly debunked since then, many scholars seem to have gone to the opposite extreme of denying that there are any differences between city and suburb that cannot be reduced to socioeconomic characteristics of the population. I take issue with that point of view.

I shall also challenge the currently popular view that local community control necessarily reinforces racial discrimination and segregation. The issue of suburb versus city is related to the issue of local community control, since a major difference between a city neighborhood and a suburb is the political autonomy of the latter. I will argue, in fact, that the effect of local control was quite the reverse of that commonly assumed—that it was the means by which Oak Park achieved to the extent it did its goal of racial integration.

However, before digressing too far from method, I must add those cautions on the limitations of our method that are de rigeur in case studies. Case studies in general and participant observation in particular have certain well-known disadvantages. Findings apply directly only to the very limited cases, although certain general arguments and propositions can be suggested. The method is sensitive to the fine grain of the phenomenon while also affording access to the larger community context; but the close-up view may obscure or exclude larger patterns and trends.

Proof and inference are always problematic in participant observation. While it is not usually feasible to put specific hypotheses to systematic tests, neither is the final interpretation limited by a research model devised at the outset. Rather than yielding specific findings, the observations are more likely to suggest interpretations. I make every effort to present the evidence accurately and completely enough so that the reader can assess the strengths and weaknesses of those interpretations.

For this study, the method chosen seemed to hold more advantages than liabilities. Research on the community response to racial change is still at the stage of generating propositions, and many dimensions of the phenomenon are still obscure. Participant-observation case studies may reveal some of them. Furthermore, this method affords a certain faithfulness to the subject that more abstract methods do not give. The patterns of change and response, of perception and redefinition, were continually evolving in the communities during the course of the observation. They could not easily have been anticipated, and usually they could not be quantified. The method chosen seemed necessary to describe in any depth the processes taking place, and it seemed the best avenue of insight into the highly subjective nature of community experience of racial change.

Nonetheless, it should be made quite clear, despite my disclaimers and my emphasis on description, that I do not consider this study devoid of theoretical meaning. I have already suggested some of the theoretically relevant issues, and I shall repeatedly return to these and others.

2

Austin: Between Slum and Suburb

In the 1930s Ernest W. Burgess and others at the University of Chicago mapped the city of Chicago into seventy-five community areas, reflecting as far as possible their residents' perceptions of community boundaries and identities. This was done as an aid to collecting and reporting social and demographic data for socially and culturally distinct subareas of the city.[1] One of these subareas, six miles from the Loop on Chicago's western perimeter, was known as the Austin Community Area. Before racial change began, most Austinites could readily identify the boundaries of their community as the Belt Line railroad tracks on the east, Austin Boulevard on the west, Roosevelt Road on the south, and North Avenue on the north. As figure 2 shows, this highly consensual definition differed from Burgess's only in that it excluded an irregularly shaped strip of land lying between North Avenue and the Chicago, Milwaukee and St. Paul railroad tracks. The western end of this area, known locally as "Galewood," is considered a distinct community. The rest of that strip of land was rather vaguely perceived by most Austinites as belonging to the Belmont Cragin Community Area that borders Austin on the north.

This area beyond North Avenue is composed of middle-class white neighborhoods characterized by neat brick bungalows and two-flats. In Galewood, locally considered a "very nice community" and a frequent choice of white emigrants from Austin, the bungalows give way to larger and newer Georgian and ranch homes. The inhabitants are likely to be white-collar or well-paid blue-collar workers, and the wide, tidy lawns and well-maintained homes lend the area a "suburban" appearance.

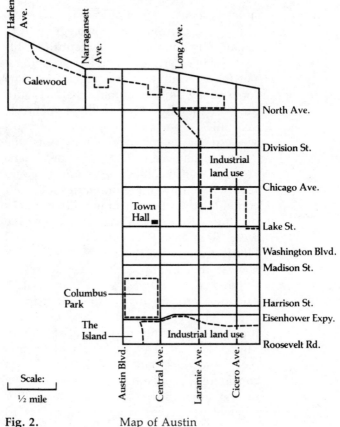

Fig. 2.   Map of Austin

Three poorer communities border Austin on the east. Humboldt Park is an ethnically mixed area where blacks and Puerto Ricans are the main groups replacing whites of Italian and Eastern European descent. South of there, North Lawndale and West Garfield Park are lower-income black communities. Directly south of Austin lies the solidly white, militantly antiblack working-class suburb of Cicero. On the west is Oak Park. Thus, until the end of the decade of the sixties Austin sat between slum and suburb, as Austinites recognized all too well, though the older residents were wont to recall earlier times when the neighborhoods to the east had been considered "good" and even "high class."

It is difficult to describe the internal geography of Austin before racial change without anticipating the effect of transition on the mental map held by Austin residents. Racial "dividing lines" were to become as important as the natural barriers of rapid transit lines, expressway, industrial districts, railroads, and major streets in providing the common symbols through which residents organized and communicated their perceptions of the community. But even before racial transition began there were some significant territorial divisions and sharply distinguished nodes of activity.

No other barrier divided the community as surely as did the Eisenhower Expressway, slicing through its southern edge and excising an area of a little less than a square mile. Most of this territory is occupied by industry, but there are a few residential blocks at both the eastern and the western ends. The area of modest homes and apartments that lines the expressway at the eastern fringe of this large industrial park acquired no distinctive identity in the eyes of other Austinites. On the western edge, however, is the little neighborhood known as "the Island." Its insularity is afforded not only by the expressway but by Columbus Park flanking the expressway on the north. The Island came to seem more like an appendage of the suburb of Cicero than a part of Austin. It formed its own local organizations and generally declined to participate in the larger Austin community life. When the rest of southern Austin became black, the Island remained white.

Although the most important commercial streets in Austin were Roosevelt Road, Madison Street, and North Avenue, with smaller businesses strung out along Chicago Avenue and Division Street, there was no question that the symbolic center of Austin was the intersection of Lake Street and Central Avenue, the original nucleus around which the present Austin community gradually developed. Located there were the old Town Hall (converted to a Chicago Park District recreation center), the YMCA, and the Austin branch of the Chicago Public Library, as well as some convenience stores. The offices of the major civic organizations were also clustered there, as were the Democratic Ward Committee office and branches of some city departments and citywide social service agencies. Not far south of the Central-Lake intersection was Austin's synagogue, and not far north was the large old fieldstone Methodist Church. The deterioration to which parts of the area had fallen victim by the late sixties failed to conceal the onetime elegance of the surrounding residential area. Many times I heard residents refer to this neighborhood as "special" because of its history and tradition, witnessed by the ornate, turreted Victorian homes set on wide streets and parkways.

History

Austin began as a commuter suburb when the Galena and Chicago Union Railroad (later the Chicago and North Western) was built in the 1840s.[2] By 1874 Austin had about one thousand residents, mostly English and native-born Americans. Many substantial businessmen built large homes in the neighborhood of Central Avenue and Lake Street, the core from which Austin was to expand in all directions.

A variety of factors contributed to the growth of Austin in the late nineteenth century. The proximity of the railroad yards and shops and of several manufacturing plants brought craftsmen to the area, though the housing was still largely beyond the economic reach of laborers. When the Chicago fire in 1871 dispersed the city's population, Austin was one of the recipients. Two street railway lines reached Austin by 1900. The population had grown to about four thousand by this time. When it was annexed to Chicago in 1899, the comfortable suburb of Austin became a choice west side city neighborhood.

Austin's greatest growth occurred between 1900 and 1930, when the entire present community was built up and population neared its peak. The development of the Lake Street elevated rapid transit line brought many more Chicago Loop workers into the community. Southern Austin grew in a fast spurt in the 1920s, when Columbus Park was completed, and large apartment buildings went up around its grassy malls. The northern part of Austin developed after the Division Street streetcar line was extended to Austin Boulevard in 1915, and growth in this section boomed in the 1920s.

The Austinites of the early 1900s were a cosmopolitan group of native-born Americans, Scots, English, Germans, European Jews, Swedes, and Irish. The Irish settlers eventually assumed the dominant role in Austin's social life. The Roman Catholic churches, with their Irish clergy, Irish religious orders in the schools, and markedly Irish culture became the hubs around which community life revolved.

During the 1930s, large numbers of Italians began moving into Austin from the more crowded and deteriorating neighborhoods to the east, and by 1960 they were the most numerous group. The Irish, however, remained the largest single foreign and second-generation ethnic group in the central area of Austin around the Town Hall, and they maintained their social and political dominance over most of the larger community, despite their minority status. However, some of the Roman Catholic churches north of Chicago Avenue became identified as heavily Italian parishes, and Italian American culture was much in evidence in these neighborhoods.

Culture and Social Organization

In Austin, ethnicity, culture, and social organization were fused. Immediately before racial change, Austin could still be aptly described as "Catholic" and "Democratic," with the capitals emphasized. The Irish still maintained the dominance they had gained and exercised through the institutions of church and political party. An Austin resident said: "Austin was an Irish dynasty. There were strong ties among the churches. There was Resurrection and Saint Kate's and Help of Christians and Siena High School—it was called Saint Catherine's Academy then. They were all Irish. The churches ran Austin."

The Roman Catholic church remained very important, and Austinites of all faiths felt its influence. The pervasiveness of Roman Catholic symbolism was seen in the way Austinites used parish boundaries as geographic reference points: they identified their neighborhoods by the churches there. Though Protestants may not have used this device as often or as readily as Roman Catholics, it was generally assumed that everyone, regardless of faith, knew what parish he lived in, for this part of community culture transcended individual religious affiliations. Whenever possible, diminutives of parish names were used. For example, Saint Thomas Aquinas and Saint Catherine of Siena churches were most commonly referred to as Saint Tommy's and Saint Kate's.

The local Roman Catholic high schools, one for girls and one for boys, were also run by religious orders of Irish origin, and ethnic socialization was as much a part of school as it was of home life, and often more so, since it touched even the non-Irish. Alumnae of the girls' high school recalled being taught jigs by the nuns. Parents with college aspirations for their children thought first of Notre Dame, and its athletic teams commanded a large and devoted Austin following. A local VFW post was named after Knute Rockne. Taverns throughout Austin had names like "Sheehy's and Sullivan's" and "Brady's," and the jukeboxes featured the Irish Rovers and Bing Crosby singing "Galway Bay."

Residents of central Austin often spent summer evenings on front porches drinking beer and chatting with neighbors into the early morning hours. Sometimes the conversation turned to tales of ghosts and hauntings originally told by parents and grandparents from the old country. But there were reputed to be some contemporary local ghosts as well. Once when I returned from an out-of-town trip, a neighbor reported that she had followed just such an otherworldly visitor up the stairs to my third-floor flat in one of Austin's typical converted Victorian houses; after it had disappeared through the locked door, she had sprinkled the stairway with holy water to bar its return.

In the face of in-migration of other white ethnic groups and finally of blacks, Irish influence waned without totally giving way. As the parishes underwent racial transition, old-style Irish priests might be replaced by younger progressives, though even many of them had Irish surnames. The girls' high school remained open until 1977, headed by nuns who had graduated from the school themselves, but it had moved to a smaller building and served an almost all-black student body one-third its former size. Many of the local politicians were still Irish, too; but remapping of city wards and of state congressional districts allowed the southern part of Austin to be conceded to black representatives.

All parts of Austin, whatever their racial and ethnic composition, have long been considered safely Democratic by the city's political powers. Systems of power and prestige in Austin were dominated by and firmly linked to the city's preponderantly Irish hierarchies of Democratic politics and the Roman Catholic archdiocese. It was within this dual framework that Austinites derived their sense of living in an "elite" community—a term often used by the older residents. There were communities in Chicago far more affluent than Austin, and the south side Irish strongholds may have had their powerful politicians, but Austin considered itself the home of the Irish judges and successful businessmen. While the Democratic political organization had Austin firmly in its control, the Catholic churches unified and solidified the community, knitting it together at the neighborhood level.

Population and
Housing Characteristics

To form an idea of Austin's population and housing stock before racial transition began, it is instructive to view the 1960

census data rather than the 1970 data. For that reason, tables 1
through 3 present figures for both years for the Austin census
tracts whose locations are shown in figure 3. Table 1 shows
that the major changes between 1960 and 1970 took place in
those tracts that had undergone racial transition in the meantime. The changes often represented reversals of the white
population trends. For example, the total population of Austin
had been declining since 1950. Although the 1970 data indicate
a population increase, tract population growth was confined,
with only one exception, to tracts that were more than 20 percent black. White Austin continued its population decline.

Fig. 3.   Austin census tracts, 1970

In 1970, almost 30 percent of Austin's residents were of foreign stock, with Italians making up the largest group (25 percent), followed by the Irish (12 percent). The British, Scandinavian, and German groups that were so prominent in Austin's early formative years had long since moved on.

In 1970 some ethnic areas were still readily identifiable, but racial change had drastically disrupted the former settlement pattern. Many of the Irish had moved from the middle of Austin to neighborhoods north of Division Street, where Italians were already concentrated. Spanish-speaking people, making up 3.6 percent of Austin's 1970 population, were found mostly along Austin's eastern border between Lake Street and Chicago Avenue, with smaller concentrations along the fringes of black ghetto expansion. A Greek residential community in southern Austin had been completely displaced by 1973. Jews, who had been one of southern Austin's major groups, had also abandoned the area, and the synagogue on South Central Avenue had been sold to a black Baptist congregation.

In 1970 Austin had a black population of 32.5 percent, almost completely concentrated south of Lake Street. By 1974 black people were living north of Chicago Avenue, and by 1977 Division Street was considered a racial dividing line.

Along with the change in the ethnic composition of the community came changes in the age structure. Austin's population had steadily aged since the climax of the community's development in the 1930s. By 1960, 13.1 percent of the residents were at least sixty-five years old, and only 25.8 percent were under eighteen, making Austin one of the oldest of Chicago's communities. The aging of the population went hand in hand with its dwindling as Austin's children grew up and left the community and fewer and fewer young families moved in to replace them. This trend continued through the 1970s in most of Austin's white neighborhoods, while in the racially changing areas the age structure shifted dramatically downward. This was to be extremely important as racial change began in the schools.

In terms of residential mobility, Austin had been moderately stable. According to the census, its residents were less prone to move than those of the city as a whole. Racial change, however, was accompanied by a sharp increase in the percentage who had lived in different homes in 1965.

Another change that took place between 1960 and 1970 was in the socioeconomic status of the population. In 1960 Austin was a solidly middle-class community. It was slightly higher than the city as a whole in median family income, school years completed, and proportion of the working population employed in white-collar jobs. Austin retained that slight edge over the rest of the city in 1970, but the census tract data in table 2 reveal a clear split along racial lines. All but two of the predominantly white tracts had median incomes higher than the city's median of $10,242, and all but one of the predominantly black tracts had median incomes lower than the city's median. However, almost all of Austin's census tracts experienced a drop in occupational status between 1960 and 1970. It may be, as others have suggested, that white-collar workers tend to leave a changing community earlier than do blue-collar workers.

As table 3 indicates, more than 90 percent of Austin's dwelling units were built before 1950. After 1930 there was very little residential construction except in Galewood. Most of Austin's units were renter-occupied, especially in the southern half of the community. For all the indicators of housing characteristics we have used, the considerable variation among census tracts makes the community area medians less illuminating than the intertract ranges. In 1970 home values ranged from $13,700 as a median in southeast Austin to more than $30,000 in the northwest corner. There was also a substantial spread in the median rents by tract: from $100 to $141.

By the 1960s Austin had reached the end of its life cycle, the point when conventional wisdom and sociological theory tell us population succession typically occurs.[3] Still, it is far too simplistic to say that the community's aging population and housing stock made Austin ripe for transition while the ghetto's proximity made it inevitable; for the very same might have been said of Oak Park, the community to which we now turn.

Austin Community Area	Total Population		Percentage Black		Percentage Foreign Stock		Percentage 65 Years and Older		Percentage under 18 Years		Percentage in Different House, 1955, 1965	
	1960	1970	1960	1970	1960	1970	1960	1970	1960	1970	1960	1970
Total or median	125,133	127,981	0.0	32.5	47.4	29.9	13.1	6.5	25.8	31.2	46.7	57.1
Census tracts												
2501	506	481	0.0	0.0	43.9	22.7	11.9	8.3	32.6	35.8	38.5	44.7
2502	2,864	2,640	0.0	0.0	48.9	49.2	10.8	14.4	29.1	27.0	39.6	37.2
2503	4,583	4,183	0.0	0.0	50.4	48.1	10.8	13.2	27.3	23.9	43.5	39.7
2504	6,244	5,795	0.0	0.0	53.6	56.7	12.5	17.4	23.8	23.8	40.2	39.3
2505	7,770	7,445	0.0	0.0	54.9	47.2	10.9	16.6	26.6	23.0	34.8	30.4
2506	4,766	4,479	0.0	0.0	46.5	45.2	14.5	16.0	28.0	29.4	31.7	43.0
2507	6,515	6,138	0.0	0.0	52.5	53.6	14.2	17.0	25.2	23.9	44.0	40.9
2508	2,907	2,742	0.0	0.0	49.2	49.7	12.7	14.6	28.0	27.3	39.8	37.1
2509	1,078	941	0.0	0.0	43.6	50.7	9.4	11.7	30.8	29.4	36.2	54.3
2510	1,619	617	0.0	0.0	50.0	53.4	11.9	11.0	27.1	24.1	48.6	52.8
2511	5,495	6,143	0.0	0.1	43.9	45.6	13.5	13.5	28.6	27.9	43.8	46.2
2512	4,746	4,557	0.0	0.1	39.6	39.1	14.3	14.5	28.6	30.3	43.2	38.5
2513	5,996	5,750	0.0	0.0	43.9	48.8	13.3	15.0	27.6	28.2	45.4	39.7
2514	5,992	5,645	0.0	0.4	41.7	41.0	15.8	16.6	22.7	23.0	50.9	57.2
2515	5,639	5,375	0.1	5.0	41.2	34.2	13.8	13.8	23.1	26.9	53.4	58.1
2516	5,164	4,823	0.0	1.1	44.5	31.4	11.6	10.7	29.8	34.2	43.9	47.7
2517	3,299	2,844	0.0	0.8	39.5	28.9	9.6	8.9	32.7	34.8	47.6	50.6
2518	9,653	10,887	0.0	91.1	43.9	4.3	13.1	3.0	25.7	41.8	55.1	83.1
2519	7,496	8,905	0.0	73.7	44.2	9.0	15.0	6.1	21.6	35.9	57.2	80.0
2520	6,874	7,229	0.0	20.4	46.4	29.0	17.7	15.6	17.8	20.9	52.0	62.4
2421	10,272	11,817	0.0	67.7	55.3	15.1	12.8	7.1	26.7	37.5	46.9	74.4
2522	11,754	14,616	0.0	95.1	48.0	2.1	11.9	2.1	24.7	40.9	54.5	77.1
2523	1,375	1,426	0.0	80.2	43.8	13.3	8.0	4.2	33.4	48.5	58.2	61.8
2524	2,526	2,503	0.0	8.1	54.6	41.8	12.7	19.2	23.7	23.5	34.6	52.6

Source: U.S. census, 1960, 1970.

Table 2 **Socioeconomic Characteristics of the Population, Austin Community Area, by Census Tract, 1960, 1970**

Austin Community Area	Percentage Male White-collar Workers		Median Family Income (in dollars)		Median School Years Completed	
	1960	1970	1960	1970	1960	1970
Median	44.5	31.2	7,602	10,766	10.6	11.2
Census tracts						
2501	—a	9.1	—a	9,667	9.1	8.8
2502	37.8	29.5	7,315	12,048	9.9	10.0
2503	38.0	33.5	7,447	11,529	9.9	10.7
2504	40.3	36.4	8,056	11,610	10.2	11.4
2505	56.9	56.4	9,984	13,853	10.8	12.1
2506	53.7	35.4	7,882	12,640	11.4	11.6
2507	43.5	34.0	7,854	11,014	10.2	10.3
2508	32.6	32.7	8,333	11,360	10.1	10.9
2509	41.8	27.2	8,000	11,750	10.0	9.5
2510	31.5	22.8	6,979	10,520	9.9	9.9
2511	40.4	31.2	7,389	11,115	10.5	10.7
2512	48.0	39.7	7,286	11,613	10.8	11.6
2513	38.6	29.5	7,711	11,264	10.1	10.6
2514	47.1	39.6	7,067	10,670	11.7	11.7
2515	43.8	38.5	7,492	10,647	11.3	11.5
2516	36.4	33.7	7,372	10,989	10.0	10.5
2517	23.2	18.4	6,887	9,984	9.2	10.2
2518	38.5	25.0	6,831	8,251	10.0	11.1
2519	54.8	29.8	7,444	9,609	11.6	11.7
2520	54.6	39.7	7,853	10,218	11.9	12.3
2521	52.7	30.9	7,876	10,927	11.1	11.9
2522	43.1	28.0	7,200	8,780	10.4	11.2
2523	31.7	21.2	6,902	8,125	8.9	10.6
2524	45.1	37.8	7,516	10,807	10.2	10.9

Source: U.S. census, 1960, 1970.

1960, 1970

Austin Community Area / Census tracts	Total Dwelling Units		Percentage Owner-Occupied		Percentage Built since 1949		Median Home Value (in dollars)		Median Gross Monthly Rent (in dollars)	
	1960	1970	1960	1970	1960	1970	1960	1970	1960	1970
Total or median	44,554	44,868	37.7	36.6	4.9	9.8	18,700	20,900	98	129
2501	160	168	41.3	36.3	—[a]	5.3	—[a]	17,000	—[a]	103
2502	880	890	57.6	57.4	8.6	11.9	18,000	21,300	96	118
2503	1,562	1,555	47.5	47.5	2.6	6.0	17,700	21,400	103	132
2504	2,147	2,150	53.1	51.5	3.7	6.8	19,100	22,900	107	134
2505	2,397	2,485	84.6	81.9	25.6	29.1	24,800	30,100	110	141
2506	1,487	1,438	64.6	65.0	1.6	2.6	19,100	21,900	100	133
2507	2,233	2,251	44.8	42.1	5.0	6.4	18,600	21,600	109	136
2508	903	908	55.5	54.4	5.9	9.3	18,200	20,500	105	128
2509	330	344	53.9	47.7	6.1	6.8	16,300	18,400	—[a]	100
2510	564	263	36.0	21.3	—[a]	3.4	16,800	17,900	95	109
2511	1,752	2,104	39.6	37.8	0.5	2.1	16,800	18,000	101	124
2512	1,532	1,484	59.8	59.2	0.3	0.7	17,500	19,000	97	125
2513	2,028	2,039	43.5	44.0	1.8	2.8	16,600	18,100	104	131
2514	2,517	2,564	22.3	18.8	1.0	5.1	17,900	18,100	91	116
2515	2,364	2,248	29.2	27.7	4.2	13.0	15,800	16,400	88	117
2516	1,677	1,585	44.7	43.8	0.7	2.4	13,700	15,200	93	120
2517	1,094	969	37.7	36.6	0.4	2.2	13,500	13,700	78	113
2518	3,650	3,402	19.4	17.3	0.3	5.9	15,800	15,900	91	130
2519	3,111	3,342	18.7	15.6	0.5	9.3	17,300	18,000	103	134
2520	3,119	3,481	13.9	10.5	2.1	18.5	19,600	19,100	105	130
2521	3,467	3,689	31.3	27.7	5.7	11.7	18,700	18,800	105	136
2522	4,284	4,241	29.1	22.7	14.9	18.5	18,600	19,000	94	137
2523	419	362	37.2	38.4	4.8	6.0	15,600	17,000	83	130
2524	877	906	40.8	37.1	2.3	4.6	17,500	20,700	94	122

Source: U.S. census, 1960, 1970.

[a]Census figures not available.

3

Oak Park: The Marriage of Old and New

Just west of Austin across Austin Boulevard lies the Village of Oak Park, a residential suburb with a 1970 total population of 62,511. Like Austin, it is situated on the Eisenhower Expressway and the Lake and Congress rapid transit lines, making travel to the Loop swift and convenient.

The boundaries of Oak Park are Harlem Avenue, North Avenue, Austin Boulevard, and Roosevelt Road, as figure 4 illustrates. Chicago neighborhoods, including Austin and Galewood, lie to the east and north. Oak Park's northwestern neighbor is the affluent suburb of River Forest, home of bankers, business executives, and, reputedly, some of the top men in Chicago's crime syndicate. Southwest and south are situated the working-class suburbs of Forest Park, Berwyn, and Cicero.

Internal divisions in Oak Park are created by the natural barriers of elevated tracks and expressway, but they are not as acutely perceived as in Austin. The Lake Street "el" roughly separates north Oak Park from south Oak Park, the northern half having generally more expensive housing and enjoying somewhat more prestige. The designation "south Oak Park" is sometimes reserved for the segment south of the expressway. As in Austin, the expressway represents the major spatial cleavage reinforcing the social differentiation that predated the expressway's construction. This southernmost part of Oak Park has the least

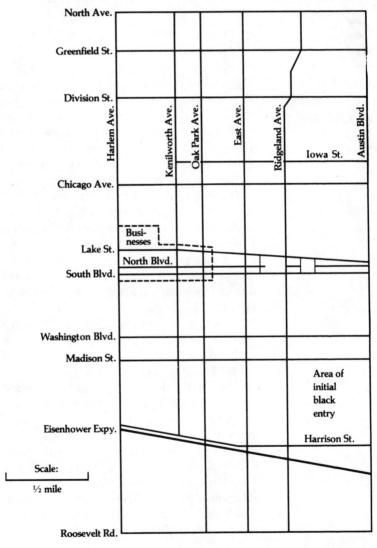

Fig. 4.   Map of Oak Park

expensive homes on the narrowest lots. An Oak Park official talked about the differences: "Some people say south Oak Park is really north Berwyn, but I don't share that view myself. The neighborhoods aren't really different north of the expressway or south of it. They were there and the housing was there long before the expressway was built. However, there are a great many people there with ethnic and employment ties that center in Cicero and Berwyn. A substantial number of people in south Oak Park work at Western Electric and other factories in Cicero.... Also, there is strong feeling against the establishment, that is, the VMA.[1] They think the VMA is all those people who live in north Oak Park—those people who live up on Greenfield.... It's not what you'd call a liberal area. It is not an area receptive to our efforts to be friends."

This split is not as sharp, however, as that between the Island and the rest of Austin. Other internal neighborhood distinctions in Oak Park are even less profound. Sense of neighborhood is vague, far overshadowed by the sense of belonging to Oak Park. Elementary-school attendance areas tend to provide internal spatial structure in much the way parish boundaries did in Austin.

There are no industrial areas in Oak Park, and only a sprinkling of light manufacturing. The major commercial strips, as in Austin, are Roosevelt Road, Madison Street, and North Avenue. The central business district extends for a half mile between Oak Park Avenue and Harlem Avenue and includes the contiguous blocks on either side of Lake Street, the main business street. In 1975 the north end of this business district was closed to traffic and converted to a pedestrian shopping mall. The condominium and apartment buildings encircling the downtown area represent the bulk of recent residential construction.

History: The Old Aristocrats and the New Progressives

In 1835 Oak Park's first settler, Joseph Kettlestrings, purchased a plot of land in what is now downtown Oak Park. There he built a tavern to serve the drivers traveling the wagon trail that passed through the area—an ironic beginning for a community that later became "dry" and remained so for more than a hundred years.[2]

Similar or sometimes the same events spurred the growth of Oak Park and Austin. The Galena and Chicago Union Railroad was constructed through Oak Park (then called Oak Ridge) in 1848. After the Chicago fire, a number of wealthy families relocated in Oak Park, bringing the population to about five hundred in the early 1870s. Fifteen years later the population had risen above thirty-seven hundred, and by 1902 it had reached ten thousand. Oak Park's early well-to-do settlers were followed by others of more modest, but in no way marginal, means. Population growth was very rapid in the first quarter of the twentieth century, and the community was solidly built up and densely populated by the time of the Depression. The population continued to grow slightly between 1930 and 1940, then declined until the 1960s, when there was a slight gain in population coinciding with a new wave of apartment and condominium construction.

Before 1900 Oak Park and Austin were both part of the Township of Cicero, and the two were bitter political rivals. Oak Park tried more than once during the late 1800s to separate itself from the rest of the township, but it was always prevented by the opposition of the Austin voting bloc. When the issue of annexation of all or part of Cicero Township by Chicago came to a vote in 1899, however, Oak Parkers found their revenge by voting Austin into the city and the rest of the township out, even though Austin's own voters were against annexation. Oak Park separated itself from Cicero Township and incorporated as a municipality in 1901.

The heated political feud in which the two communities engaged was paralleled by a competition for prestige. Though like Austin in many ways, Oak Park was always Austin's social better. It was farther out from the center of the city, it was richer, and it had a distinct air of moral superiority. Its cherished status as a "temperence community" and its many churches earned it the nickname "Saints' Rest." The Unitarians were an influential group, and their Unity Temple was Frank

Lloyd Wright's first commission for a public building. Nearby, on choice downtown property, the handsome edifices raised by the early Presbyterians, Congregationalists, and Lutherans still stand.

What Oak Parkers may have considered righteousness, however, was as likely to be called snobbery by Austinites and other neighbors. When it was suggested that Austinites looked upon Oak Parkers as "aristocrats" who wore "ruffled nightshifts," an Oak Park village father retorted that "the dwellers in 'Saints rest' do not run about nights to see what kinds of night shirts other people were wearing and hence were not familiar with the *robe de nuit* of their Austin neighbors."[3]

In 1974 a local newspaper columnist wrote, "I grew up in Berwyn and Cicero, which really isn't pertinent except to explain a conversation I had recently with an old neighbor. I was telling her about how exciting it is to be a part of Oak Park as it faces the challenge of racial change. But she was unimpressed. 'I recall when we were young we thought Oak Park was filled with snobs,' she said sarcastically, 'So now it will be filled with black and white snobs. What's the difference?'"[4]

Culture and Social Organization

Betty Van Wyk, a young reporter for the Oak Park newspaper *Oak Leaves,* was interviewing one of the village's innumerable "lifelong residents" when the old lady asked her, "And you, my dear—were you born here?" No, said Betty. "Oh, toooooo bad," sighed the lady. And her sympathy couldn't have been more genuine if Betty had described a childhood as a sickly orphaned waif.

That's Old Oak Park: snug, secure and confident that on these shady streets and inside these thick stucco walls is absolutely the finest of lifestyles.[5]

The cultural atmosphere and imagery so well captured by a Chicago journalist in the passage quoted above set Oak Park apart from its neighbors and from other western suburbs far more than did its objective physical and demographic characteristics.

By the 1960s Oak Park's relative prestige among Chicago's

western suburbs had declined considerably, a combined effect
of the aging of its housing stock and the rapid growth of newer
and more expensive developments farther west. But there was
something more to Oak Park's identity that could not be expressed in measures of wealth. Its image as a well-established,
affluent, white Anglo-Saxon Protestant community remained
remarkably durable despite some contrary demographic trends.
Within its immediate surroundings, Oak Park did stand out
from the blue-collar, ethnic suburbs of Cicero, Berwyn, and
Forest Park. Even much wealthier River Forest compared with
Oak Park, from the point of view of Oak Parkers, as the
nouveaux riches to the aristocracy, fraying though that aristocracy may have been.

Part of Oak Park's special aura can be traced to its historical
and cultural roots, most visibly preserved in its architecture. In
the compact section of north Oak Park known to the zoning
board and real estate dealers as the "residential estate" district,
north and east of the shopping mall, several blocks are lined
with large, sumptuous homes, many worth more than $100,000
even before housing prices became so inflated in the 1970s. One
of the grandest of Oak Park's old residences and part of the
grounds of another that has been torn down have been preserved as parks, and the Park District also owns two of the
oldest homes in Oak Park.

Frank Lloyd Wright built his own home and studio in Oak
Park, and there are more than two dozen other homes there that
he designed entirely or remodeled. A large part of north Oak
Park was designated a historic preservation district because of
its architectural heritage, including the Wright homes and more
than forty other buildings of major architectural significance.[6]

Wright was not Oak Park's only favorite son. The boyhood
home of Ernest Hemingway, still standing, received a special
dedication during Oak Park's 1974 Hemingway festival. One
cannot stay long in Oak Park without being made aware that
the village was once the home of Hemingway and Wright, not
to mention Edgar Rice Burroughs, who wrote some of his Tar-
zan novels while living in Oak Park. Apparently the present
generation of Oak Parkers are less offended than their

forefathers by Wright's eccentricities, and they have forgiven Hemingway his reference to Oak Park as a town of "wide lawns and narrow minds."

What is important here is that the image of community held by Oak Parkers and promoted through the local media rested far more on such things as its expensive homes, architectural landmarks, quality stores,[7] favorite sons, and a few affluent citizens than it did on any average measures or objective criteria of housing and population characteristics. One would be greatly misled by mere census reports.

Oak Park's atmosphere of quality was further enhanced by its high level of cultural activity: a local repertory theater; an opera company; a symphony orchestra; a well-attended annual lecture series; an art fair; a modern, well-stocked library; and other similar homegrown aesthetic offerings. Although the metropolis had grown up around it, Oak Park remained something more than a convenient dormitory for Loop workers. It was still a village in its own right, with its own institutions and its own culture.

By 1970, significant inroads had been made by what was frequently called the "new Oak Park": younger, progressive, involved, and issue-conscious. Nevertheless, the social life of Oak Park was still heavily influenced by the upper strata. The Oak Park Club, the Oak Park Country Club, the Nineteenth Century Club, and many service fraternities and sororities received prominent coverage in the social pages of the local press. *Oak Leaves,* the local newspaper with the largest circulation, was almost an official organ for the community, striking the balance between "old Oak Park" tradition and "new Oak Park" progressiveness, a blend that community leaders also tried to project. Actually, the distinction between "old" and "new" Oak Park was less a cultural split among its residents than a change in imagery. Oak Park's oldest leading families were found among the most avid backers of the "new Oak Park" style.

Most residents probably belonged neither to "old" or to "new" Oak Park. For them, Oak Park was a community of homes, schools, and churches, and a family centered, suburban life-style that was sharply distinguished in their minds from the

central city's way of living. The quest for purity expressed in
the temperence movement in the late 1800s and in "blue laws"
in the early 1900s reemerged in Oak Park in the 1970s in the
form of the anti–high-rise movement. High-density residential
zoning became one of the most controversial issues in years and
gave expression to intense antiurban sentiments. One man
protested angrily: "I ran away from Chicago. I ran away from
high rises. I ran away from pollution. I ran away from crime . . . .
A high rise will never be built in Oak Park—I will bet my shirt
on that!" Another equated high rises with moral laxity: "We'll
have people swinging in and swinging out. I don't have anything against swingers: I just don't need them in my neighborhood."

On one occasion a local official informed a public meeting
that Oak Park already had more apartments than single-family
homes. A general murmur of protest and denial immediately
arose. The audience refused to believe him, though he was
absolutely correct.

Most Oak Parkers were proud of Oak Park's heritage, comfortable with its way of life, willing to admit the need for
change yet afraid of that change. As one man put it, "We're in
favor of change, but stable change."

The suburban imagery was also reflected in Oak Park's
reform-style politics. Since 1953 Oak Park had had a village
manager form of government. Six trustees and a village president were elected every four years in a nonpartisan, at-large
election. The Village Manager Association, a loosely knit coali-
tion, completely dominated municipal politics. It had won
every election since its formation in 1952. The Village Manager
Association became directly involved only with electoral politics. It lapsed into inactivity—some people even said
nonexistence—after every local election. Its continuity was provided by a loose core of leaders. There was little consensus in
Oak Park over what individuals, groups, or interests, if any,
held the balance of political power. Most people seemed to
think the decision-making structure was quite fluid, dominated by a common culture rather than by any particular individuals or organizations. When asked who had power, people

might mention certain specific groups or prominent families, but there was not much agreement among the people questioned, and most were strikingly reluctant to say that anyone had real political power in the village.

The village government enjoyed considerable prestige and respect. "Good government" and official integrity were assumed without question. Those elected to local office were almost invariably business and professional people (though not typically of the local business community) and were thought of as such, not as politicians.

In county, state, and national elections, Oak Park cast a Republican majority vote, but the margin was steadily narrowing. The Republican and Regular Democratic Organizations had precinct organizations that were weak by city standards, but the Independent Democrats were strong enough to be taken very seriously by candidates for office. In 1974 Independent Democrats won the election for party committeeman and the primary race for state congress over regular organization incumbents. A candidate for state office in a district that included Oak Park talked about the suburban political style as contrasted with the Chicago neighborhoods included in the same legislative district: "In my few forays into Oak Park, I've noticed a strange phenomenon. Once having crossed Austin, it is chic to become independent as opposed to Democratic. I've run into people out there who were some of my best Democrats in the city. Now that they've moved to Oak Park they claim to be independents . . . . Politics—big city politics—is anathema."

The League of Women Voters was one of Oak Park's more influential organizations. When asked about the league's reputed power, one of its members, who also held an important village government post, smiled and replied with a very affirmative "Uh-huh." Then she continued: "Just about every village commission has at least one Leaguer on it. Some people don't think it should be that way, but that's the way it is."

By 1974 the "new Oak Park" spirit was being reflected in official local politics in a very conscious and deliberate manner. Its bywords were professionalism and progress. It was a style of action that was aggressive rather than reactive and that was

innovative in using the most up-to-date methods of management and planning. At least this was held up as the ideal, even
if actual practices sometimes fell short.

Population and
Housing

Many of Oak Park's housing and demographic characteristics
seemed to contradict the prevailing image of the community, as
we can see in tables 4 through 6. But particular note should be
taken of the large intertract variations on some of the indicators.
These variations are more striking in Oak Park than they were
in Austin. Figure 5 locates the census tracts referred to in tables
4 through 6.

Like Austin, Oak Park was originally settled by English, Germans, and Scandinavians, but whereas population succession
transformed Austin into an Irish Catholic stronghold, Oak Park
retained much longer its image of Anglo-Saxon Protestantism.
Many longtime Oak Parkers remembered when discrimination
against Jews, Catholics, and Southern or Eastern Europeans in
general was common in the village.

Germans were still the leading nationality in 1960, but by
1970 they had been supplanted by Irish and Italians. Most of the
population, however, was made up of third- or later-generation
descendents of foreign immigrants, with only 30.2 percent of
them being either foreign-born or of foreign or mixed native and
foreign parentage. Obviously we must take care in interpreting
census data on ethnicity, since the census does not trace European descent beyond the second generation in America. We
therefore know nothing about the ethnicity of most Oak Parkers
(or Austinites, either, for that matter) who are not classified
among the foreign-stock population, and to say that the numbers or proportions of certain groups declined means only that
the first and second generations decreased absolutely or relatively. The way people identify themselves is clearly more important than the way the census identifies them, and ethnic
identification of any sort did not appear to be as strong in Oak
Park as in Austin.

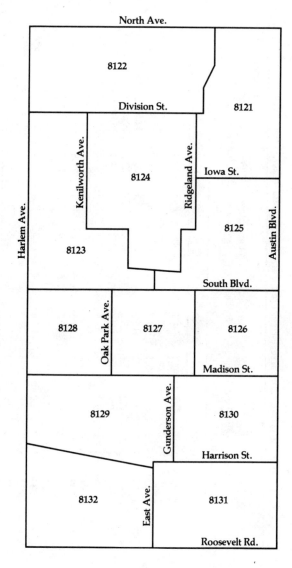

Fig. 5. Oak Park census tracts, 1970

Table 4   Selected Population Characteristics, Oak Park, by Census Tract, 1960, 1970

Oak Park	Total Population		Percentage Black		Percentage Foreign Stock		Percentage 65 Years and Older		Percentage under 18 Years		Percentage in Different House, 1955, 1965	
	1960	1970	1960	1970	1960	1970	1960	1970	1960	1970	1960	1970
Total or median	61,093	62,511	0.1	0.2	34.3	30.2	14.9	16.3	27.2	27.8	42.8	45.6
Census tracts												
8121	5,322	5,293	0.0	0.1	38.7	37.4	15.3	16.7	28.6	28.9	31.7	40.7
8122	4,503	4,578	0.3	0.1	41.8	37.6	12.9	15.1	28.1	30.5	32.5	33.0
8123	5,692	6,014	0.2	0.1	35.2	33.7	17.0	22.8	22.3	19.7	52.2	60.3
8124	4,130	4,495	0.4	0.6	25.3	23.6	13.2	12.9	34.1	36.0	41.2	50.1
8125	4,494	4,439	0.0	0.3	32.4	29.0	15.4	16.1	23.7	23.6	48.1	48.0
8126	4,564	4,566	0.0	0.1	32.2	33.2	19.2	20.6	20.7	22.2	45.0	42.2
8127	3,509	4,096	0.0	0.5	25.5	26.5	15.5	15.2	25.8	24.9	51.8	52.1
8128	5,752	6,266	0.1	0.1	37.0	32.5	17.9	22.3	16.8	14.9	59.1	60.2
8129	6,421	6,531	0.0	0.1	32.5	24.2	13.8	12.2	32.3	34.7	37.0	43.3
8130	5,533	5,477	0.0	0.3	32.4	22.3	13.7	12.1	32.4	36.6	40.9	39.0
8131	5,832	5,481	0.0	0.3	39.3	33.3	12.7	13.5	29.6	29.2	39.3	40.2
8132	5,341	5,275	0.0	0.0	34.6	28.7	13.1	12.9	31.4	33.6	36.4	33.9

Source: U.S. census, 1960, 1970.

Whereas Protestants had once outnumbered Roman Catholics by two to one, the majority of in-migrants to Oak Park in the early sixties were Roman Catholic, and the two groups were about evenly split by 1967.[8] By 1976 Roman Catholics outnumbered Protestants, mkaing up 52 percent of the religiously affiliated population compared with the Protestants' 40 percent. The remaining fraction was divided among Jews, Greek Orthodox, and other religions.[9]

The 1970 census came too early to gauge Oak Park's changing racial composition. In 1960 Oak Park's fifty-seven black residents for the most part represented a declining servant population. The increase in black population in 1970 was largely the result of the modest successes of an energetic fair-housing contingent. But by 1976 blacks numbered more than three thousand.[10]

Oak Park's population, like Austin's, had been aging, reaching the end stage of a population life cycle by 1960. But after 1960 an influx of younger families, many fleeing ghetto expansion on the west side of Chicago,[11] brought the median age down from 40 in 1960 to 36.7 in 1970. Yet the percentage of residents in the older age categories remained very high.

Oak Park's population was only slightly more residentially stable in 1960 than was Austin's. The highest mobility rates, higher than in any part of Austin before racial transition began, occurred in tracts where there was new apartment construction.

Three conventional indicators of socieconomic status are displayed in table 5. The differences in social class measures between Oak Park and Austin were more striking than differences in most of the other indicators of population characteristics. The table shows that Oak Park's people were relatively well educated, and more than two-thirds were employed in white-collar jobs in 1970. The median family income of $13,823 was not extraordinarily high, but it was at least $2,000 higher than in most Austin tracts, white or black. One should note, however, the much higher status of census tracts 8122 and 8124. These neighborhoods had much to do with the prestige Oak Park as a whole enjoyed.

Most of Oak Park's housing stock was at least as old as Aus-

Table 5   Socioeconomic Characteristics of the Population, Oak Park, by Census Tract, 1960, 1970

	Percentage Male White-collar Workers		Median Family Income (in dollars)		School Years Completed	
	1960	1970	1960	1970	1960	1970
Oak Park						
Median	70.1	68.8	9,131	13,823	12.5	12.8
Census tracts						
8121	69.3	60.6	8,986	12,902	12.3	12.5
8122	88.7	90.1	17,006	21,321	12.9	13.9
8123	74.6	73.1	9,257	14,399	12.7	12.9
8124	80.9	82.4	14,442	19,805	14.1	14.9
8125	69.6	62.8	8,535	13,199	12.6	12.7
8126	68.6	71.2	8,762	12,538	12.5	12.7
8127	79.8	74.8	10,033	14,918	12.8	13.3
8128	69.9	70.7	8,313	13,957	12.6	12.8
8129	69.2	66.5	9,012	13,420	12.4	12.7
8130	67.8	63.3	8,831	13,517	12.3	12.8
8131	50.5	57.2	7,910	11,668	11.3	12.3
8132	62.5	58.0	8,239	12,514	12.1	12.4

Source: U.S. census, 1960, 1970.

Table 6   Selected Housing Characteristics, Oak Park, by Census Tract, 1960, 1970

Oak Park	Total Dwelling Units		Percentage Owner-Occupied		Percentage Built since 1949		Median Home Value (in dollars)		Median Gross Monthly Rent (in dollars)	
	1960	1970	1960	1970	1960	1970	1960	1970	1960	1970
Total or median	21,555	23,206	49.1	45.5	6.1	16.5	21,500	26,200	114	156
Census tracts										
8121	1,722	1,771	78.3	75.9	1.9	6.6	20,300	25,300	122	145
8122	1,370	1,409	89.3	85.9	23.4	26.0	25,000+	43,100	—a	181
8123	2,462	2,671	30.7	30.0	8.1	23.9	22,500	28,200	120	172
8124	1,209	1,334	76.5	71.7	3.3	8.0	25,000+	37,300	132	173
8125	1,575	1,721	37.3	34.3	6.0	13.4	21,500	28,200	110	146
8126	1,879	1,993	24.5	20.8	1.6	9.5	22,400	27,500	116	149
8127	1,365	1,683	28.4	22.8	15.2	36.2	25,000	30,900	130	182
8128	2,760	3,355	13.3	12.2	5.9	28.8	24,400	28,000	116	161
8129	1,917	1,958	66.5	63.0	2.9	5.9	20,200	23,900	108	146
8130	1,651	1,626	64.9	63.4	3.1	6.2	18,800	22,900	113	153
8131	1,953	1,989	57.3	55.6	2.5	4.9	17,100	20,800	103	134
8132	1,692	1,696	62.9	63.9	4.1	6.7	18,500	22,800	106	138

Source: U.S. census, 1960, 1970.

aCensus figures not available.

tin's, but Oak Park experienced a small boom in apartment and condominium construction during the 1960s. There was practically no internal open space for new development, and since Oak Park was hemmed in by other suburbs most future development would have to be upward. In 1973 the foundation was dug for a twin-tower, thirty-seven-story apartment building. But by 1977, because of community opposition to high rises as well as financial difficulties on the part of the developer, who ultimately defaulted, the project had progressed no further than a gaping hole.

Most of Oak Park's housing was in rental units, not typical for a suburb of its age. What gave Oak Park its deceptively homeowning appearance was the fact that single-family homes occupied 79 percent of the residential land. The largest single category of dwellings comprised structures of six or more units. These large apartment buildings occupied only 5 percent of the residential land and were concentrated along south Oak Park's main thoroughfares and around the central business district.[12]

In general, Oak Park's housing stock was more costly and in better condition than Austin's. But again the intertract variation was very large. It is more pertinent to compare south Oak Park, the area in the path of racial change, with south Austin. In 1960 the differences between these portions of the communities were slight.

Although Oak Park's homes were old, the market for them continued to be very strong. It was frequently said that their structural soundness and internal craftsmanship made them attractive bargains for young couples willing to do some work on them. Yet the same might have been said of central Austin's once lovely Victorian Queen Anne homes; but in 1977 whites were still avoiding that market.

From similar beginnings Austin and Oak Park took divergent paths—Austin locked into the city's social and political hierarchies and Oak Park developing an autonomous, reform style of government and diversified bases of influence and prestige. Austin exprienced a typical pattern of population succession, which Oak Park managed to forestall until the 1950s. The clearest differences in population and housing in the two communities were in characteristics closely related to social status. These included the cost of housing as well as the measures presented in table 5. The Oak Park community was of generally higher status than Austin. That is, not only were Oak Park's residents of higher status, but the community itself enjoyed greater prestige. Austinites may at one time have thought of their neighborhood as elite, but Oak Parkers frequently pointed out that their own suburb's reputation was national or even international.

Yet these differences were never great enough to prevent a meaningful rivalry from developing between the communities and continuing over several decades. Nor were they great enough to afford much comfort to white Oak Parkers when the neighboring community underwent racial transition. It was common to hear Oak Park residents say that Austin had been "just like Oak Park" before the change.

4

Two Patterns of Change

Whatever the differences between Austin and Oak Park, white residents eventually came to share the same fear: that Chicago's massive black ghetto would continue the seemingly inexorable expansion that had caused one after another west side neighborhood to change from all white to all black, and that the same fate would befall Austin and Oak Park.

Transition in South Austin

In 1964 only the Belt Line railroad tracks separated Austin from a black residential area that was more than six miles wide in places and extended all the way to the Loop. Even more than the railroad tracks, however, Cicero Avenue, two blocks west of the tracks, was coming to be perceived by Austin's white residents as the boundary between black- and white-controlled territory. White Austinites commonly remarked in retrospect that nobody thought "they" would cross Cicero.

"It can't happen here"—familiar expression born half of hope and half of fear—was as prevalent and as wrong in Austin as anywhere. Cicero Avenue was not a "dividing line" for long, and each of the successive boundaries that divided Austin between white and black gave way as easily.

The growth of black population in Austin is shown in figure
6, and the progress of block by-block change is summarized in
table 7. In the four years between 1966 and 1970, 148 blocks
changed from white to black occupancy, an average rate of 37.0
blocks per year. Between 1970 and 1973, an estimated 113 more
blocks changed occupancy, a rate of 37.7 blocks per year, extending the black sector of Austin north to Chicago Avenue. By
1975 many blacks lived between Chicago Avenue and Augusta
Boulevard, two blocks north, and total turnover seemed inevitable there as well.

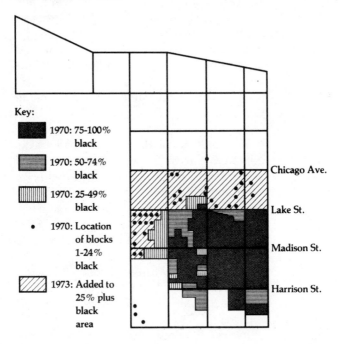

Fig. 6.   Growth of Austin's black residential area, 1970–
73. Sources: U.S. census, block statistics; Real
Estate Research Corporation estimates.

The pace of territorial expansion of the black community in
Austin was apparently steady over the seven-year period.
However, the neighborhoods north of Lake Street, which ex-

Table 7   **Pattern of Growth of Austin's Black Residential Area (Blocks 25 Percent or More Black), 1966–73**

Year	Length of Peripheryᵃ (city blocks)	Area (residential census blocks)	Rate of Expansion (blocks per year)
1966	6	0	—
1970	14	148	37.0
1973	21	252	37.7

Sources: 1970 from U.S. census, block statistics; 1966 and 1973 from on-site observation and Real Estate Research Corporation estimates.

ᵃThis includes northern and western peripheral blocks only, i.e., those along the vector of expansion. Southward expansion was blocked by a large area of industrial land use.

perienced racial change after 1970, had generally lower housing densities than the neighborhoods south of Lake Street. This means that the rate of transition of dwelling units must have slowed even though the turnover of blocks remained fairly constant. Perhaps this is because the higher proportion of renter occupancy in the neighborhoods south of Lake Street made them more susceptible to racial change. The extension in length of the "front" of ghetto expansion that also occurred over this period apparently had no effect on the speed of expansion. There was evidence of some "leapfrogging," but none of the white blocks that were skipped over held out for long. The differences in population or housing characteristics that may have made blocks more or less susceptible to change were obscured by the persistent pace of racial transition. The pattern of racial change that had become classic in Chicago neighborhoods was surely being repeated in Austin.

Dispersed Black Residence in Oak Park

Would the "Chicago pattern" hold for a suburb as well? The answer most consistent with the urban ecological tradition is that mere political boundaries would prove irrelevant to the course and effect of an ecological process and that, indeed, suburbs adjoining large areas of black residence would become extensions of the black community. Oak Park provided the Chicago area's first real test case, and its experience turned out to be far different from the transition that most urban ecologists would have predicted and that had actually been predicted by more than one Chicago urbanist and reported in the local press.

The ghetto first became contiguous to Oak Park at the village's southeast border, between Madison Street and the Eisenhower Expressway. Upon reaching the city limits, however, the main thrust of ghetto expansion shifted northward. The neighborhoods north of Lake Street in Austin thus became largely black before any part of Oak Park experienced much transition. In Oak Park in early 1973, only the string of small apartment buildings along Austin Boulevard south of Madison Street were more than 25 percent black, whereas most of the Austin blocks between Lake Street and Chicago Avenue had become at least 25 percent black. In the summer of 1974 most of the remaining white residents were moving out of that area of Austin, but Oak Park still had very few predominantly black blocks, and whites continued to move into all Oak Park neighborhoods.

Table 8 shows the pattern of growth of Oak Park's black population by geographical quadrant, using East Avenue and South Boulevard to divide the suburb into four areas of approximately equal size. Black in-migration was increasing, but it was still much slower than in Austin. In the two years between the end of 1971 and the end of 1973, about fifteen hundred black people had moved into Oak Park residences, while certainly several times as many had moved into Austin.[1]

In 1974 Oak Park's black population was still less than 3 percent, and in 1977 it had grown only to 8 percent, according to the estimates of the Oak Park Community Relations Department, which obtained its information from landlords, real estate brokers, and other observers.

In 1977 Oak Park leaders were encouraged by the apparent stability of those blocks of single-family homes in the southeast

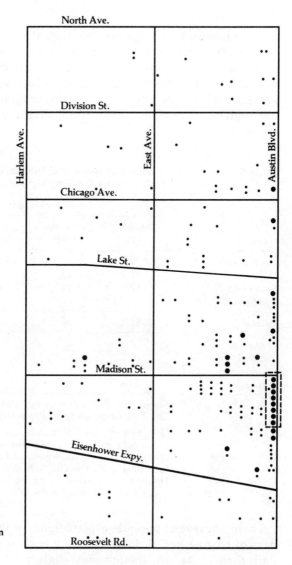

Fig. 7. Approximate location, within one square block, of black and interracial households in Oak Park, August 1973. Source: Oak Park Community Relations Department.

quadrant, which had seemed perilously near "tipping" four years earlier. But in some large apartment buildings change continued. On the other hand, there were apartment buildings where the trend toward racial change had actually been reversed. This was most likely to happen, though, when a building underwent complete renovation, displacing the previous tenants.

Table 8   **Number of Black and Interracial Families in Oak Park by Geographic Sector, 1971–73**

	Date of Count			
Sector	March 1971	December 1971	August 1972	August 1973
Northwest	9	11	15	16
Northeast	11	13	19	46
Southwest	10	14	19	36
Southeast	21	49	91	187
Total	51	87	144	285
Average monthly gain (since last count)	—	4.5	7.1	11.7

Source: Oak Park Community Relations Commission; Oak Park Community Relations Department.

Note: In 1970, the U.S. census enumerated 5 black heads of households in the northwest sector, 6 in the northeast, 4 in the southwest, and 8 in the southeast, for a total of 23. The Oak Park Community Relations Department estimated that there were between 400 and 450 black families in the village in April 1974.

There are several possible explanations for the relative slowness of change in Oak Park. Housing was more costly in Oak Park than in Austin, though only slightly so in the southern portion. Probably the dearth of mortgage money that hit the real estate industry in 1973 played a large role in retarding racial change throughout the area. Such economic factors were no doubt important, but they hardly account for all of the difference. Although they may partially explain Oak Park's slow rate of change, in no way can they explain its most important departure from the "Chicago pattern": the dispersal of black residency throughout the community.

In 1972, 38 percent of Oak Park's black and interracial families lived outside the village quadrant adjacent to the heavily black area of southern Austin. A year later that figure had declined to 34 percent. That is, two-thirds of Oak Park's black residents were concentrated in southeast Oak Park; but, more important, one-third were not. We can see from a glance at figure 7 that the constricted block-by-block pattern of change that characterized Austin was absent in Oak Park.

In 1977 Oak Park could not confidently be called a racially stable, integrated community. Its rate of black population growth, if projected indefinitely, would certainly end in an all-black community. Whether that projection is warranted depends on many incalculable events and developments external as well as internal to the community. But with white demand for housing continuing strong, there seems no justification for labeling Oak Park a transitional community.

The Oak Park case does incontrovertibly show that we cannot continue to rely on the invasion-succession model as our exclusive paradigm for racial change on the ghetto's periphery and that, contrary to what researchers have found in other places,[2] community reaction to impending change may significantly affect the outcome.

Property Values and Housing Costs

Racial change, actual or anticipated, is commonly believed to affect property values in a neighborhood. Oddly enough, two contradictory beliefs are current, and both have received some support from social scientists. One belief is that racial change lowers property values; and while most research has found that this is not true, at least in the long run,[3] a recent study of the Chicago housing market found that blacks generally paid less than whites for comparable housing, lending some credence to the popular belief.[4]

On the other hand, some people have held that blacks pay

more than whites for comparable housing—a "color tax"—
because racial discrimination restricts the supply of housing
available to them. This belief has also found impressive support
in the scholarly literature.[5]

To test such perceptions against market realities, we analyzed
median selling prices for all single-family homes in Austin and
Oak Park that underwent title transfers from 1968 through
1972.[6] The results were entirely inconclusive. Over the five-year
period the median prices did not actually decline in any tract,
whatever its racial characteristics or proximity to the ghetto. In
some tracts, however, the increases during the period were so
slight that, measured against inflation, the real values had actually gone down. There was extreme variation in Austin's black
and changing tracts, some of them showing the smallest price
increases and others some of the highest. Thus there was no
evidence to support either the proposition that racial change
depreciated property values or the idea that blacks paid a color
tax, for in some of the black and changing tracts prices went up
substantially compared with the rest of Austin and in others
they went up very little.

Oak Park, of course, had no black or clearly changing tracts,
but we could find no relationship there between proximity to
the ghetto and the rate at which median home prices rose.

A different story emerged, however, from data taken from the
1960 and 1970 censuses on changes in median rents by tract in
Austin. (Oak Park was not included here, since no substantial
racial change had occurred by 1970.) Table 9 shows that the
southern Austin census tracts, which had undergone complete
or partial transition by the time of the 1970 census, had larger
rises in median rents over the decade than did most of the tracts
that remained white. Of the ten tracts with the greatest rent increases, all but one had experienced some racial transition. The
four predominantly black tracts ranked first, second, fourth, and
seventh in magnitude of median rent increases among the
twenty-four Austin census tracts. This was definitely not because the housing stock in these tracts had been upgraded by
new construction—only fourteen new structures had been built
during the decade in the tract that experienced the greatest rent
increase.

Table 9   **Median Gross Rent and Percentage of Change, Austin, by Census Tract, 1960, 1970**

Census Tract and Racial Character	Median Gross Monthly Rent (in dollars)		Percentage Increase 1960–70
	1960	1970	
White			
2501	—[a]	103	—[a]
2502	96	118	22.9
2503	103	132	28.1
2504	107	134	25.2
2505	110	141	28.2
2506	100	133	33.0
2507	100	136	26.0
2508	105	128	21.9
2509	—[a]	100	—[a]
Fringe			
2510	95	109	14.7
2511	101	124	22.8
2512	97	125	28.9
2513	104	131	26.0
2524	94	122	29.8
Changing			
2514	91	116	27.5
2515	88	117	33.0
2516	93	120	29.0
2517	78	113	44.9
2520	105	130	23.8
Black			
2518	91	130	42.9
2519	103	134	30.1
2521	105	136	29.5
2522	94	137	45.7
2523	83	130	56.6

Source: U.S. census, 1960, 1970.

[a]Census figures not available.

The method used here is not particularly sophisticated, but the results do tend to favor the "color tax" theory. When blacks find their housing costs inflated beyond those of whites, it is because there exists a "dual housing market" in which the housing supply for blacks is rigidly separated from that available to whites. Blacks can gain housing outside of the ghetto only when entire blocks on the ghetto's edge are transferred from the white to the black sector of the market.[7] This inevitably leads us to consider the policies, practices, and institutional arrangements that perpetuate the dual housing market—the subject of the next chapter.

5

Real Estate and Lending: The Mediating Institutions

Neighborhood racial change is mediated through the individuals and institutions that operate in the real estate market—those involved in real estate sales, rentals, and mortgage lending, to name a few of the most important functions. Merely to carry on their routine business, actors in these institutions must make decisions concerning local communities, and they base these decisions in part on their perceptions and definitions of the present characters and probable futures of those communities. The central, mediating roles the real estate institutions play in the process of residential turnover—and therefore racial turnover—make their operating definitions and the perceptions and actions of their agents extremely significant in determining the fates of communities.

The Lenders

One of the findings of the National Academy of Sciences—National Academy of Engineering Advisory Committee to the Department of Housing and Urban Development in 1972 was that "Mortgage financing institutions have had separate lending policies for blacks and whites. They have been timid in developing policies for realizing mixed residential areas."[1] A manifestation of that timidity has been the reluctance of lenders to grant conventional, or noninsured, mortgages in nonwhite and changing neighborhoods. This has meant that the Federal Housing Authority's Section 203 and, to a lesser extent, other governmental or private mortgage insurance programs have become nearly the only means of financing home purchases in neighborhoods which the lenders have defined as "changing."

In the same year, a prominent black real estate broker estimated that 90 percent of black home buyers in Chicago received federally insured mortgages.[2] The overwhelming majority of these purchases were made in areas already black or soon to become black.

The refusal of lenders to grant conventional mortgages in racially changing areas, known as "redlining," has had multiple implications and interpretations. Many white residents have come to equate FHA (Federal Housing Authority) mortgages with black in-migration. Signs proclaiming "FHA go away" and "FHA, we're here to stay" have appeared in the windows of homes in many Chicago neighborhoods, and it is apparent that for these people "FHA" has become a code word. FHA in any form, accompanied by redlining or not, has become despised in white neighborhoods with black communities nearby, and neither Austin nor Oak Park was an exception. There was strong sentiment in both communities in favor of drastically limiting the number of FHA mortgages to be granted there.

In addition to the belief that FHA mortgages bring black residents into previously white neighborhoods, thus hastening their transition, other criticisms have been founded on the charge that FHA loans permit the purchase of older homes by marginal buyers who cannot afford to maintain them. This criticism was frequently heard in Austin and Oak Park, and it had some credibility in view of the age of most of the housing in those communities.

Finally, redlining has an important symbolic meaning for a community. It is a sign for all that the neighborhood is "going." Powerful and influential interests have lost faith in it, and that stands as a warning to any home-seekers or commercial investors to look elsewhere if they have the means to do so.

As Austin underwent racial change, residents reported that conventional loans were more difficult to secure, whereas FHA-insured loans were plentiful. In 1974 a representative of a local community organization gave his view that almost all the loans being made south of Chicago Avenue in Austin were guaranteed by FHA, regardless of the financial ability of the buyer. Though his organization was active in housing issues, he knew of no conventional loans being made in this part of Austin.

On the other hand, lenders denied that redlining was being practiced in Austin. The president of one savings and loan firm placed the following advertisement in the June 1973 issues of the weekly newspaper the *Austinite*:

> I would like to dispel another rumor that there is no conventional mortgage money available in Austin for mortgages. This is definitely a rumor and not true. In the year 1972, Austin Federal made 151 conventional mortgages and rejected only 14, and during the first five months of 1973, we made 80 conventional mortgages and rejected 9.

However, statistics compiled by the Society of Real Estate Appraisers (SREA) on the numbers and locations of FHA and conventional mortgages in 1971 tell a different story. The SREA data showed that of 204 mortgages granted south of Chicago Avenue, all were federally insured. Between Chicago Avenue and Division Street, there were only 4 conventional mortgages out of a total of 27, and between Division Street and North Avenue there were 9 conventional mortgages out of 22. It is important to remember that in 1971 blacks had just begun to move north of Lake Street. The area between Lake Street and Chicago Avenue was still predominantly white, and the neighborhoods north of Chicago Avenue were virtually all white, with residents believing them to be "safe" for the time being, since Chicago Avenue was then perceived as the racial dividing line. Significantly, in the sector of the Austin Community Area from North Avenue to the northern border, an area not perceived by local residents as actually a part of Austin, 62 out of 63 mortgages recorded by SREA were conventional.

Data obtained from the FHA itself for the subsequent years of

1972, 1973, and 1974 reinforce the impression left by the SREA figures. Of 2,010 section 203 mortgages in the Austin Community Area in those years, 99 percent were south of North Avenue, and 95 percent were south of Division Street.

Neighborhood organizations throughout the city, including Austin's Organization for a Better Austin, had made vigorous attempts to persuade lending firms to disclose their home loan records. They pressured the Federal Home Loan Bank (FHLB), the regulatory agency for the savings and loan business, to make disclosure mandatory and to take punitive action against redliners. Although the FHLB refused to compel disclosure, aided by Northwestern University's Center for Urban Affairs, they conducted a survey of savings and loan firms in Chicago and selected suburbs, including Oak Park, asking for the number and dollar amounts of conventional and insured mortgages by zip code. Out of 189 firms approached in the voluntary survey, 127 returned fully completed questionnaires.

This survey revealed a far more favorable picture of lending practices in Austin than was portrayed by either the SREA or the FHA data. It tended to support the local lenders' claims that conventional mortgage money was indeed available in Austin. But looking at table 10 we see again that the northern section of Austin was almost devoid of FHA or VA (Veterans Administration—a mortgage insurance program for veterans similar to FHA) loans. It is also important to observe that in zip code 60644, which takes in all of Austin south of Chicago Avenue, the number of loans reported represents only a small fraction of the total housing transactions and therefore of the total number of loans that must have been made there, though not necessarily made by the firms responding to the survey. Racial change was taking place rapidly in the blocks just south of Chicago Avenue during the period covered by the survey.

None of these data actually prove redlining in Austin. The purpose of the FHA section 203 program was to enable families with lower incomes and limited savings to purchase homes with low down payments. If none of the applicants met the normal credit criteria for conventional mortgages, the granting of insured mortgages only could not be construed as redlining.

Table 10   **Type of Mortgages, by Zip Code, Austin and Oak Park 30 June 1971–30 June 1973**

Location (zip code)	30 June 1971–30 June 1972			30 June 1972–30 June 1973		
	Conventional	FHA/VA	Number of Firms	Conventional	FHA/VA	Number of Firms
North Austin [a] (60635)	193	0	32	145	0	55
North Austin [a] (60639)	482	1	47	462	0	65
Central Austin [a] (60651)	129	25	31	160	2	54
South Austin (60644)	19	22	15	30	2	49
Central Oak Park (60301)	122	2	12	135	0	26
North Oak Park (60302)	86	12	21	152	7	38
South Oak Park (60304)	81	69	16	118	15	32

Source: Federal Home Loan Bank.

[a] Approximately one-half of zip codes 60635, 39, and 51 lie outside the Austin Community Area.

Redlining occurs when conventional loans are denied because of characteristics (especially racial) of the neighborhood where the property is located rather than because of the borrower's lack of qualifications. But the evidence presented here at least strongly suggests that unless FHA was present to make the venture virtually risk-free, lenders tended to seek investment opportunities elsewhere than in south Austin.

The FHLB survey also showed that FHA loans in Oak Park were concentrated in the southern half, the area most susceptible to racial change. These survey figures came as something of an unpleasant surprise in Oak Park. Although there had at least been suspicion that redlining was going on there, there was never quite as much anxiety over the issue as in Austin.

In late 1971 the Oak Park Community Relations Commission had surveyed forty new homeowners and found only two with complaints about the treatment they had received from lenders. Even these complaints could not be substantiated upon further investigation. A second survey of Oak Park real estate brokers, undertaken on the premise that brokers would steer their clients to the lenders with whom they had the least difficulty, thus shielding the buyers from awareness of dubious practices, also brought to light no evidence of redlining.

In 1972 the Oak Park Citizens' Action Program (CAP) also conducted a survey of new home buyers, particularly those who had purchased homes in southeast Oak Park. The first fifty such calls found the new residents satisfied with their dealings with the lending firms. The survey continued in a rather more haphazard fashion for a year, but with the same results.

CAP then began telephone "testing" of the local savings and loan firms. The CAP caller would identify himself as wishing to sell an Oak Park home and would attempt to solicit some statement from the lending institution official regarding the mortgage possibilities. Responses, however, tended to be vague, as lenders refused to be pinned down to specific statements on the basis of the general information given them. After some prodding, an official of one of the firms allegedly conceded that his company would probably "go conventional" in Cicero and Berwyn and FHA in Oak Park. This was the go-ahead for CAP to initiate a major campaign against redlining in Oak Park.

The local lending firms responded by creating an organization called Financial Institutions Special Committee for Area Leadership (FISCAL), through which the four local banks and four savings and loan firms that made up the committee agreed to release data on the type and location of mortgages they granted. An analysis by type and geographic zone of the mortgages made by FISCAL members from July 1972 through June 1973 is presented in table 11. The zones were derived by dividing the village into four roughly equal parts along South Boulevard and East Avenue. The southeast zone, of course, was the one community leaders considered "'sensitive."

Table 11   Actions taken on Mortgage Applications to FISCAL Members, by Location, July 1972– June 1973

Location	Mortgages Granted		Mortgages Rejected
	Conventional	Insured	
Northwest	42	0	10
Northeast	40	5	11
Southwest	58	2	12
Southeast	64	16	25
Total	204	23	58

Source: Financial Institutions Special Committee on Area Leadership, Oak Park, Illinois.

The data provided by the FISCAL lenders indicated that conventional mortgages were still available in southeast Oak Park. In fact, more were granted there than in any other location. On the other hand, southeast Oak Park had more insured mortgages than the three other zones combined. It also accounted for a disproportionate share of the mortgage application rejections.

Although CAP's antiredlining campaign was first directed at local lenders, the group later charged that some major downtown Chicago firms were also redlining. CAP was not alone in this opinion. According to a spokesman for one local real estate brokerage, it was common knowledge in the business that some Chicago firms redlined all or part of Oak Park, and real estate agents simply did not bother to refer buyers to them.

The presence of large numbers of FHA loans in Austin soon began to be obvious. The many black residents who had given their newly purchased homes needed repairs, paint jobs, siding, and other improvements could only be sorely frustrated when boarded-up, foreclosed homes began to be evident. In 1975 it came to the attention of the Oak Park village government that Oak Park had also had two FHA foreclosures, setting off a new wave of alarm among local officials. But in Austin two such foreclosures on a single block was not uncommon.

As important as the withdrawal of mortgage money was, it was not immediately visible. Of more direct emotional effect was the physical flight of the lending firms themselves. In April 1973 two Austin savings and loan companies announced plans to open suburban branches: Laramie Federal Savings and Loan in Schaumburg, and Austin Federal Savings and Loan in Bloomingdale. Both were new and fast-growing western suburbs, far removed from Austin. Although these moves were opposed by Austin groups as soon as the news was released and were interpreted by Austinites as showing the firms' loss of faith in the community's future, both companies denied any intention of permanently withdrawing from Austin. Despite such reassurances, however, within a few months after it opened, Laramie Federal Savings and Loan in Schaumburg began operating under the name First Federal Savings and Loan, and the Austin Location became known as the "Laramie branch" of the First Federal. In other words, the proposed Schaumburg "branch," had become the main headquarters.

In Oak Park, one of the largest of the local savings and loan firms was denied permission by the Federal Home Loan Bank Board to open an office in a far western suburb, maintaining the Oak Park facility as a branch. The move had been fought bitterly by Oak Park community groups, opposed, as in Austin, as much for the symbolic damage as for the objective finanacial harm it might do.

Thus, commitment of mortgage lenders to the community
was problematic in both Oak Park and Austin, and the threat
was always present that the viability of the communities would
be undercut by redlining. It is safe to say, when we have pieced
together that fragmentary data presented earlier in this chapter,
that Austin was substantially redlined, while in Oak Park the
suspect practices were at least less prevalent, though not entirely absent. Most local firms and some downtown Chicago
firms evidenced their continued support by making conventional home loans in all Oak Park neighborhoods. A major reason for the difference was that Oak Park was never clearly
defined as a "changing neighborhood," as was Austin. The
operating definitions used by the lending firms themselves are
of crucial importance, but they are not made in a vacuum. Perceptions and definitions of change or stability arise from many
quarters and tend to have interactive effects. In Austin, this
interaction took the form of mutual reinforcement: the only
doubts that Austin was in transition apparently lay in the
minds of a few hopeful residents. This was far from true in Oak
Park, where, as succeeding chapters will show, the definition of
the situation was far more nebulous.

Real Estate Practices

Not long after racial change began, Austin became a target of
widespread panic-peddling. White homeowners were besieged
by real estate firms with telephone calls, door-to-door solicita-
tions, and mail offers to sell their homes. Residents became
increasingly concerned about the many new real estate operations that had arisen in the area, apparently seeking to reap the
profits of racial change. Local reports claimed the number of
brokerages serving Austin had jumped from less than fifty to
almost three hundred.

In May 1970, after much citywide publicity and constant local
pressure, salesmen of two real estate firms in the area had their
licenses revoked—a most unusual event. But by August they
were again doing business as usual in Austin. The license of the
president of one of the firms was suspended for two years. The
president of another firm had his license revoked. Yet a new

license was issued to him the very day after the revocation. Apparently word of the revocation had not reached the city collector's office, where the license was issued. That real estate company went out of business in November 1970, but it was soon replaced by a firm with another name but the same management. This firm closed down in May 1971 only to reemerge under yet another name. Such was the real estate business in Austin.

A series of *Chicago Tribune* articles that appeared in August 1971 contained some extraordinarily candid remarks by some of the Austin brokers:[3]

> "We don't care if the whites run all the way to Hong Kong, as long as they run . . . . I go where the money is. I'm a money-oriented guy. It's good business for us when they're frightened."

> "Chicago Avenue is the demarcation line right now . . . . No I don't know how they form . . . . But one of these days some black will move in north of Chicago Avenue. When one of them jumps, that's the green light. Then it's open season."

From my field notes comes this local clergyman's explanation of panic-peddling in Austin: "They go to the homes of these little old Irish widows and scare them into selling cheap. One guy turned over one hundred buildings all by himself."

Despite such commonly held beliefs, however, we must be skeptical of that prevailing folklore that lays the primary burden of causing racial change at the door of the panic-peddler. There were too many reports of panic-peddling in Austin for one to believe it did not exist. But those reports were often repeated second- and thirdhand, and residents hardly needed panic-peddling salesmen to tell them that racial change was possible and even likely. There were many other sources of perceptions of imminent change. Furthermore, as Molotch pointed out and I reiterated earlier, the dynamics of the dual housing market are such that racial transition would certainly occur, with or without panic-peddling, as long as real estate industry gatekeepers saw to it that whites leaving the neighborhood were replaced only by blacks.

One of the primary motives attributed to the panic-peddlers was to resell the cheaply acquired homes to blacks at inflated prices, thus reaping handsome short-run profits. To determine the prevalence of the practice, we checked the housing transfer files at the University of Chicago Center for Urban Studies for cases in which Austin homes had changed hands more than once between 1968 and 1972. These data are presented in table 12. Although the jump in price at the second sale in Austin's black tracts suggests that very profitable speculation was at least possible, there were far too few cases to permit any conclusions about the role and influence of the speculator. A very important gap in our data was the absence of homes sold on contract, for which the title is not actually transferred until the last payment is made. This type of financing is believed to be very common in black communities. Thus, we suspect we may have missed a large proportion of home sales in south Austin.

I will have more to say about the role of the real estate broker in racial change. For the time being it is enough to note that the Austin real estate situation got wide metropolitan coverage by the press and television. Though it was not unlikely that the prevalence and effects of blatantly unscrupulous practices were exaggerated, Austin became notorious for the kinds of real estate activities described above. Whatever the direct effect of panic-peddling, the profuse reporting of such practices might well have contributed to the definition of Austin as a "changing" neighborhood. The Town Hall Assembly, the more conservative of Austin's two major community organizations, maintained continually that the media attention to real estate practices in Austin created a negative image of the community that was extremely detrimental to any efforts to stabilize it.

Whether or not overt panic-peddling and blockbusting were widespread, a dual housing market clearly operated in Austin. Brokers adhered to the perceived racial dividing lines and steered whites away from black or changing neighborhoods, while they showed homes to blacks only in those neighborhoods. In the case of *Seaton* v. *Sky Realty*, the defendant (which had advertised "If you want to be a former neighbor fast, call Sky Realty") was found by the federal court judge to have discriminated racially by refusing to sell a home in northern Aus-

tin to a black couple. The evidence in the case showed that files
kept by the firm were coded to indicate the race of the client so
that it could be matched with the location of the listing. Local
fair housing leaders felt this was far from an isolated case.

Table 12		Price Increases of Austin and Oak Park Single-family Homes Sold Twice, by Location, 1968–72			
Location	Number	Mean Price, First Sale (in dollars)	Mean Price, Second Sale (in dollars)	Mean Number of Years between Sales	Annual Percentage Increase in Mean Price
Austin white tracts (2501–9)	21	27,285	29,995	2.1	4.7
Austin fringe tracts (2510–13)	4	22,250	25,125	2.1	6.1
Austin changing tracts (2514–17, 20)	9	15,722	21,500	3.0	12.3
Austin black tracts (2518, 19, 22, 23)	5	13,900	21,500	1.6	34.2
Oak Park, all tracts	23	29,717	31,109	1.9	2.5

Source: University of Chicago, Center for Urban
Studies, real estate transfer files.

Oak Park, on the other hand, was not deluged by "outside"
brokers, and it experienced very little of practices that might be
considered panic-peddling. Still, local leaders were far from
complacent. A village official put it this way: "It's a field ripe to
be raked . . . . Chicago west side realtors milked Austin, and now
some have succeeded in getting listings in Oak Park."

To Oak Park's advantage, however, it had its own local real

estate board and multiple listing service. Members were required to have offices in either Oak Park or River Forest. As the
larger of the two communities served, Oak Park was the
backbone of their business. The Oak Park market was not easily
penetrated by outsiders as long as the residents in general did
not panic. Outside brokers who were seriously trying to break
into the Oak Park housing market found it necessary to use
some special ploy, most frequently the promise of a quick sale.
For example, a black broker who had previously operated in
Maywood, another western suburb with its own large and expanding ghetto, moved into a new office across the street from
Oak Park and began soliciting Oak Park homeowners with the
promise that he could sell to cash buyers within thirty days. But
such cases remained the exception and accounted for little of the
Oak Park real estate business.

Although the outside broker was a nagging fear and a cause
for extra watchfulness by Oak Park community leaders, the
threat never materialized. As a matter of fact, the specter of the
outside broker was even useful on occasion in helping local
officials justify regulatory measures that were unpopular with
the local real estate industry.

By and large, the members of the Oak Park Board of Realtors
were sometimes cooperative and generally manageable. But
there were still problems. Some leaders thought Austin had
represented the last stand of overt blockbusting and panic-
peddling. They were of the opinion that these practices in their
earlier, more blatant forms had all but died out, only to be
replaced by the more subtle and less detectable policy of racial
"steering." "Steering" meant that real estate salespeople discouraged white prospects from viewing homes in certain areas
because the neighborhood was said to be changing.

That some Oak Park brokers practiced steering was more than
a suspicion: virtually all Oak Park leaders were firmly convinced. None of the real estate board officers denied it, and in
1973 one publicly voiced the opinion that as many as 50 percent
of the local brokers were doing it. But evidence good enough to
take to court was difficult to obtain. In 1974 a River Forest
broker was the first to be prosecuted for steering in Oak Park,

although he was acquitted. It was a reflection of the relatively open state of the Oak Park single-family home market that this was only the second formal discrimation complaint involving the sale of a home since both local and federal fair housing laws were passed in 1968. In 1975 a suit was filed in federal court against six firms from neighboring villages, alleging that they steered their white clients out of Oak Park.

During this time there were no cases involving local brokers, and by 1975 the real estate situation had shown general improvement. The housing industry had just begun to recover from a slowdown, and mortgage money was again readily available, though at much higher interest rates than before. Yet relatively few Oak Park homes were on the market, according to local real estate people, and competition for them was fierce. It was common in the summer of 1975 for a home to be sold within a week of being listed for sale and even to be bid up above its listed price. One informant, who had real estate contacts through her occupation and was very knowledgeable about the local real estate situation, said that the single-family home blocks near Austin Boulevard were more racially stable than they had been since change began. She said: "Two years ago those people on five- and six-hundred South Humphrey and Taylor were desperate to sell, and they were sure they were going to have to sell to blacks. Now they have no trouble finding white buyers." A real estate salesperson confirmed this observation: "Young couples come to us now and say, 'We want a house in Oak Park.' Two years ago they said, 'We want a house in Oak Park, but we don't want to live near Austin.'"

By 1977 the local leaders' major complaint about Oak Park's real estate brokers was that they were not practicing "affirmative marketing" vigorously enough; that is, they were not making any extra effort to sell east Oak Park homes to white buyers, though they were no longer steering them away. Even this criticism, however, did not apply to all firms.

Thus, the behavior of real estate brokers in Oak Park hardly conformed to the commonly held view that they did their best to promote racial change so they could profit from high volume or speculate for dramatic returns on their own investments.

Even in Austin, where this view was more prevalent than in Oak Park, it was at least a gross oversimplification.

To better understand the role of brokers, it is instructive to try to view the situation from their vantage point. Rose Helper's survey of Chcago real estate brokers provides some insights into their ideology, self-image, and motivation.[4] She found that few brokers were interested in "turning" neighborhoods from white to black. The typical broker saw himself as a professional and as a local businessman. As a professional he had an obligation to serve his client's interests first and to develop the expertise to guide the client in matters beyond his full comprehension. As a professional, he was also committed to a body of ethics and beliefs. As a local businessman, he depended upon satisfied customers to continue to bring him word-of-mouth business. His reputation was his major asset and his best form of advertising.

For these reasons, Helper's respondents claimed that they would not "bust a block" by selling to the first black family. On the other hand, if the broker advises potential sellers that racial change is imminent and would lead to depreciation of property values, he is only repeating in good faith what his training has led him to believe. And if he tells a prospective buyer that a house would not interest him because it is in a "changing" neighborhood or because the local school is integrated, the broker is, in his own view, acting responsibly in overseeing the interests of his white clients. This does not imply that such attitudes and behaviors ought not to be changed; it simply means that we need not ascribe ulterior motives to them.

Typically, the real estate broker has an interest in neighborhood racial stability and homogeneity rather than in change and heterogeneity, for he needs to preserve his local market, his base of operations. The real estate firms that can profit most from racial change can do so because of the way their operations are structured. One such type of firm is the large organization with many branches. This firm has a market that is geographically extensive and ethnically diverse, and without much difficulty it can open and close branches to gain the greatest volume of business. A second type, at the other end of the size continuum, is the "shoestring" operation. This real estate dealer travels light, sometimes moving from storefront to storefront as the area of transition shifts, but sometimes even operating without an office.

The black broker is in an especially difficult position. He cannot deal in white neighborhoods because he cannot attract a white clientele. He can do little business in black neighborhoods because of the low volume of home sales there.[5] Therefore he must often work the transitional neighborhoods, where he is especially vulnerable to charges of panic-peddling just because of his own color. He is also liable to run afoul of antisolicitation laws, which forbid brokers to approach homeowners who have formally registered their desire not to be solicited for the sale of their homes, for he depends upon solicitation to acquire listings. When a black broker working in Oak Park out of an office just across Austin Boulevard was charged with violating the Oak Park antisolicitation law, he filed countercharges of racial discrimination. The charges against him were upheld and the discrimination charges dismissed, in both cases by default, when his attorney repeatedly failed to appear in court.

This does not mean that the Austin and Oak Park residents' suspicions of the brokers were groundless. That the profiteering broker is a deviant type in the profession is little comfort in the changing neighborhood to which disproportionate numbers of such operators may be attracted. This was probably the case in Austin.

Yet in Oak Park, where the practices that plagued Austin were held to a minimum, the brokers' tendency toward conservatism when faced with an unfamiliar and ambiguous situation was potentially just as serious an obstacle to stable racial integration.

The exclusion of blacks from Oak Park by the gatekeepers in the real estate industry was an extension of a long tradition of equating quality with homogeneity. Before there was any question of blacks'—other than those in the clearly subordinate roles of domestics—living in Oak Park, white ethnic groups had found the door closed to them. Said one real estate man, "I remember after the war when people were shocked when they found out that we were going to have Italians living here." A longtime Jewish resident recalled that "ten or fifteen years ago it was very, very difficult for a Jew to buy a home in Oak Park." A man of Russian descent reported with lingering bitterness that before he bought his house, twenty years earlier, his neighbors "took a vote" to determine whether he should be admitted to the neighborhood. Two Roman Catholic religious orders reportedly had purchased institutional property in Oak Park only with difficulty.

Brokers in Oak Park assumed, probably accurately at the time, that residents would give little support to integration. For a while in the mid-sixties, before the passage of Oak Park's fair housing law in 1968, the Oak Park Board of Realtors cooperated with the Oak Park–River Forest Committee for Human Rights, a voluntary civil rights association, in designating certain listings that, at the request of the seller, were to be available without reference to race or creed. No more than 10 percent of the listings at any one time were formally available on this basis, and not all brokers cooperated in showing even this 10 percent to minority-group prospects.[6]

When Oak Park passed a fair housing ordinance in 1968, it seemed to the real estate professionals that the village government was requiring them to behave counter to the ethics and dogma of their profession. For example, the notion that racial and ethnic heterogeneity depressed home values had been routinely taught in real estate textbooks for years.[7] Now Oak Park brokers were being advised by community leaders and official community relations workers that this was untrue. Furthermore, they were being asked to help change the attitude of the public when they were hardly sure what to think themselves.

At a village-sponsored seminar for real estate professionals, community volunteers, and others interested in housing, a real estate salesman in the audience rose to respond to assertions by panel members that racial integration did not depress property values. Speaking very emotionally, and with obvious support from much of the audience, he asked village officials: "If that's true, why don't you educate the people? You put the burden on us. People are scared to death. For the average man, his home represents the bulk of his assets. What are you doing to educate people so that they can feel a little security?" On another occasion, a real estate saleswoman probably articulated the feelings of many of her colleagues when she said, "It's hard to sell real estate today. We've had to completely turn around in our thinking."

At least one Oak Park real estate broker did try to assume some of the educational responsibility the village had thrust upon his profession. He made frequent appearances at block club and civic meetings, where he answered questions and presented a promotional slide film produced for his firm. At one block club meeting, when the issue of home values arose, he characterized the matter as simply one of "supply and demand." Therefore, he pointed out, the only reason property values might go down when blacks moved in was if white neighbors panicked and "flooded the market with homes for sale." Even then the depression would be only temporary. This was a fairly faithful representation of the belief that local community relations people were attempting to promulgate. When I interviewed the same broker some months later, however, he described how he cooperated with the local government's policy for dispersing black residence throughout the village, but his representation of the issue of home values took a decidedly different cast than it had at the earlier meeting: "There are a great number of us who believe in the theory of dispersal, and we've been able to talk to the above-average black who comes here and say, 'on the basis of experience of other communities, if you go block by block, say you buy a home for $20,000, it's going to be worth a lot less.'"

It is hardly surprising that a broker would behave in such an ambivalent manner, given the conflicting nature of the information available to him. While the local fair housing supporters mustered a parade of experts who denounced the "myth" of declining home values, entirely contradictory claims came from equally credible sources. An example was the lecture by a Chicago urbanologist that took place in a southeast Oak Park

church hall. He compared Oak Park with a Chicago neighborhood that had undergone racial transition: "South Shore is really going down the drain, and it's a very wealthy area....
There's one area of South Shore where a lot of people live, called
Jackson Park Highlands. It's a very wealthy area, but you can
get a home there that you'd pay $100,000 for here in Oak Park,
for $30,000."[8]

Furthermore, homeowners and home-seekers often concurred
with the brokers that a broker might be acting irresponsibly
if he did not inform the prospective buyer of the racial composition or the anticipated racial stability of the neighborhood into
which he contemplated moving. For example, one woman who
sold a home in one of Oak Park's "fringe" blocks to a white
family said she would have felt guilty except that the family had
previously lived in Oak Park and therefore "knew what they
were getting into." Another resident vociferously objected to a
feature article on Oak Park's integration effort in a Chicago
daily newspaper, for, as he interpreted it, the article might
mislead people into moving to Oak Park on the dubious assumption that the community was racially stable.

Thus the brokers were caught in what they perceived as a
tangle of conflicting moral, ethical, legal, and business obliga-
tions. Community officials explicitly asked brokers to put first
what the officials defined as community interests. In fact, a
meeting between the Community Relations Commission and
the president of the real estate board broke down on just this
point. Some of the commissioners adamantly insisted that the
board president acknowledge verbally the priority of the community's welfare over any possibly conflicting business or professional concerns. The board president, however, refused to
acknowledge any obligation other than to the "principles of the
real estate profession," even though he repeatedly denied that
there could be any conflict between these principles and the
community's best interests. What the commission wanted and
at that time failed to get was an explicit assurance that they were
all playing the same game.

Moreover, local and federal laws did not request but required
behavior that often ran counter to the brokers' convictions. The

prohibitions against steering, for instance, required in effect that they withhold information that was, in their belief and often in reality, relevant to the client's housing decision. Though local and federal provisions tended to be similar or identical, the anxiety and confusion within the local real estate industry were compounded because the village board often seemed on the verge of passing ordinances that conflicted with federal legislation. The proposed, though never enacted, "quota ordinance," which would have made it a punishable offense to sell or rent housing to blacks in designated areas of the village, was a notable example. When the Community Relations Department asked for a local law requiring that real estate firms record their clients' race, brokers protested that if they did so they would be subject to prosecution under federal law. Actually this was probably not true, since federal courts had even required such record-keeping by firms convicted of bias, but the local brokers were well aware that racially coded records had been damning evidence in some successful housing discrimination prosecutions.

But although the Oak Park real estate dealers' adjustment to the new demands was often uneasy and uncomfortable, the important point is that they did adjust. However ambivalent their own feelings, they did, for the most part, comply with the demands of the fair housing law, and they attempted, at least to a degree, to cooperate in pursuing the objectives of the community leaders who were working toward integration. The compliance of the brokers and lenders was due in part to the successful tactics of pressure and persuasion exerted by community leaders, a matter to be taken up in a later chapter. But the behavior of the brokers may also be attributed to the fact that, in the end, integration served their interests. The Oak Park brokers were not for the most part fly-by-night opportunists, nor were they connected with major metropolitan real estate firms. If Oak Park could not remain a white community, then their only hope of maintaining their accustomed market was to join the other community leaders in striving for balanced integration.

It is most often alleged that fragmentation of the real estate

market into small, local institutional networks is a primary obstacle to housing integration, and usually this has been a valid
charge.[9] Local real estate boards and multiple listing services
have used their near monopolies on local housing markets to
exclude minorities. This certainly happened in Oak Park before
the community's alternatives were reduced to either becoming
integrated or becoming mostly black. But once that perception
took hold Oak Park had a better chance to achieve integration
precisely because there existed an institution through which
local real estate firms dominated the market, effectively
excluding those firms best able to profit from racial change.

6

Neighborhood Schools and Community Institutions

Real estate and lending institutions have undoubtedly had the most direct effect on neighborhood change, but others are also important. This chapter deals with those nodes of activity that are the very life of the community—the schools, churches, businesses, and similar institutions that shape the community's identity, carry on its necessary business, and forge the links that hold it together. A visitor learns much about a community by scanning the signs in shop windows or noting the particular mix of educational, religious, and fraternal organizations. Likewise, the residents learn about themselves as a collectivity when their individual purposes take them into these shared community places.

Neighborhood Schools and Racial Change

It would be difficult to overstate the importance of the schools in the local residents' evaluation of their neighborhood. If Downs is correct in his contention that middle-class whites seek cultural hegemony and thus numerical dominance above almost everything else in their residential environments, this must be doubly true of the schools to which they send their children.[1]

Even residents without school-age children cast a sharp eye toward the changing school enrollment figures that were published from time to time in the local press. Even more salient was the evidence they themselves gathered as they watched the youngsters on their way to and from school. The concern for racial balance in the schools that the childless and the empty-nesters shared with the parents of schoolchildren (even when they only talked about it without participating in school affairs) expressed a feeling that the schools represented a general community good (or bad). On these grounds, Oak Park real estate people vigorously supported each school bond issue that came up for vote. The perceived correlation of school quality with neighborhood quality was also illustrated by the anxiety that public school parents showed over the fate of the parochial schools. For example, when it seemed certain that an Austin parish school would have to shut down (as it eventually did), a committee of public school parents met with the Catholic school leaders to seek possible areas of cooperative action to keep the school open. Although the meetings were fruitless, they reflected the public school parents' assessment that many white families would leave the neighborhood if there were no alternative to the local public school, which by that time had a large black enrollment.

Since white residents recognized the role the schools played in racial change, it is not surprising that many also saw in them a hope for racial stability. As naive as it may seem in retrospect, many white Austinites believed that Austin might have resisted racial transition had the Chicago Board of Education not altered the Austin High School attendance boundaries to include some of the blocks east of the Belt Line Railroad tracks, two blocks east of Cicero Avenue. That alteration took place in 1964. The high school's black enrollment rose from one in 1963 to eighty-four the following year. Each succeeding year brought greater increases, reflecting not only the changed attendance boundaries, but also the beginnings of the migration of black families into Austin and the withdrawal of white students from the school and white families from the neighborhood. By 1972 Austin High School was virtually all black, even though there were still many white children living in its attendance area. A newspaper commented on this ironic situation:

While defiantly fighting the influx of more blacks into the
north half of Austin, the whites who live there are just as
defiantly refusing to send their children to almost all-black
Austin High School. In a kind of chicken-or-egg confusion,
Austin High School is all-black because practically none of
the 1,200 to 1,400 white children who live in its district go
there. Instead, many of them falsify addresses to go to out-
of-district schools, or if they're lucky, they go with the Board
of Education's blessing to "receiver schools" under the permissive transfer program, or if they're Catholic (as many
are), and if their parents can afford the tuition, they go to a
parochial high school.[2]

The Chicago Board of Education operated specialized vocational and technical high schools in addition to its general
academic high schools such as Austin High. For Austin boys,
Prosser Vocational High School was a feasible alternative to
Austin High, but it was closed to girls. Austin, with its traditional home- and family-centered values, seemed unlikely to
become a locus of women's rights activities, but this is just
what happened as community groups waged a successful fight
to make Prosser coeducational. Although the campaign was
couched in the rhetoric of equal rights, there seemed little
doubt that the real attraction of Prosser was not its curriculum,
but its predominantly white racial composition. Austinites also
persuaded the Board of Education to open Lane Technical High
School to their children, who had formerly been out of the Lane
district.

As table 13 shows, the rapid racial transition of Austin High
School was matched in the public elementary schools. (Fig. 8
shows the locations of the schools.) The reason was not simply
the abandonment of the schools, if not the neighborhoods themselves, by the whites. The incoming black families had more
children than the white families they replaced, and these children were more likely to attend public schools. In 1970, children
under eighteen years of age represented 39 percent of the
population of the five Austin tracts that were by then predominantly black,[3] compared with 25 percent in those same tracts
ten years earlier. Even these figures, however, fail to reflect the

Table 13   Black Enrollments of Austin Public Schools South of North Avenue, 1967–73

School	Percentage Black						
	1967	1968	1969	1970	1971	1972	1973
Austin High School	38.7	48.6	73.5	90.0	94.8	97.8	99.0
Austin Middle School I	—	—	—	—	—	99.9	99.8
Austin Middle School II	—	—	—	—	—	—	97.4
Elementary schools							
Armstrong	—	—	—	—	—	99.6	99.6
Byford	0.3	1.0	0.5	1.5	3.6	11.9	25.9
Clark	—	—	—	—	5.3	7.9	7.0
DePriest	—	—	—	—	98.7	99.4	99.8
Emmet	1.1	20.3	67.0	—	99.7	100.0	100.0
Emmet North	—	—	—	97.4	99.3	99.5	100.0
Hay	0.0	0.0	0.0	0.0	1.8	3.9	24.9
Howe	0.2	0.5	5.7	17.5	54.7	89.5	96.2
Key	0.0	0.8	8.0	20.1	50.8	86.4	97.1
Lewis	0.3	1.1	0.8	0.8	0.7	0.0	0.1
May	83.9	95.8	99.1	99.7	99.8	99.8	99.9
Nash	1.2	1.3	2.1	8.0	37.7	71.9	86.3
Spencer	82.4	90.8	97.1	98.8	99.3	100.0	100.0
Young	13.3	13.0	12.0	10.1	9.0	6.8	5.6

Source: Board of Education, Chicago Public Schools, "Racial Survey: Student," 1967–73.

Note: Absence of figures means the school had not yet opened in all cases except Emmet, 1970, for which data were unavailable.

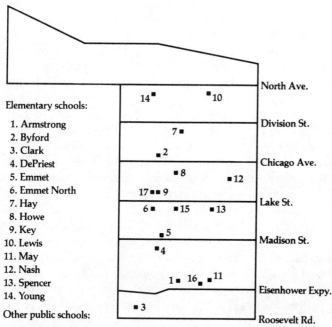

Elementary schools:

1. Armstrong
2. Byford
3. Clark
4. DePriest
5. Emmet
6. Emmet North
7. Hay
8. Howe
9. Key
10. Lewis
11. May
12. Nash
13. Spencer
14. Young

Other public schools:

15. Austin High School
16. Austin Middle School I
17. Austin Middle School II

Fig. 8.   Location of Austin public schools

real increase in school-age children, for the total population of
these tracts had also grown by 18 percent. The population increase coupled with the change in age distribution meant that
there were, in fact, 84 percent more children under eighteen in
the predominantly black tracts in 1970 than there had been in
1960, when the tracts were all white. According to the census,
the actual number enrolled in kindergarten through high school
rose from 6,452 in 1960 to 12, 207 in 1970. Moreover, these children were more likely than their 1960 counterparts to be enrolled in the public schools. In 1970, 90.3 percent of the children
in kindergarten through high school attended public schools,

compared with 54.3 percent in 1960. All told, these five south Austin tracts sent 7,520 more students to the public schools in 1970 than they had ten years before.

Even though two decades of population decline had left some Austin schools with unused classrooms, this drastic increase in the public school population more than took up that slack, and racial transition was soon accompanied by severe school crowding. With differences of race, class, and culture compounded by crowding, white parents viewed the public schools in increasingly negative terms and, as the enrollment figures demonstrate, hastily made other arrangements for their children. For many, these were simply interim arrangements pending relocation in another neighborhood.

Racially changing schools were not, then, merely a by-product of neighborhood change in Austin; they were very much the bellwether. Transition in the public schools outpaced transition of the surrounding neighborhoods. For instance, Hay and Byford elementary schools were north of Chicago Avenue and therefore north of any neighborhoods with substantial black populations in 1973. Yet both these schools had 1973 black enrollments of about 25 percent. To be sure, these black students lived within the attendance areas of the two schools, but turnover in the neighborhood can be reflected very quickly in large jumps in proportions of black children enrolled in the schools.

This point can be further illustrated by comparing the proportion of black public school children in the area with the proportion black of the total population, as is done in figure 9. Neighborhoods with less than 25 percent black population still had more than 25 percent black public school children. The area in which the proportion black among the public school children came to exceed 25 percent was always about two blocks ahead of the area in which the total population had reached 25 percent black.

We are, of course, describing a self-perpetuating cycle: increasing percentages of black schoolchildren placed increased pressure toward racial change on the immediate neighborhoods, and as the neighborhoods changed transition in the schools accelerated even more.

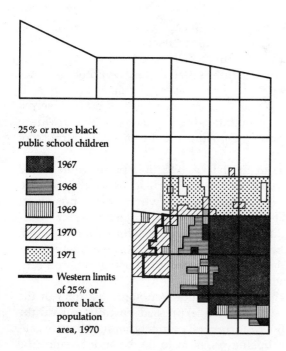

Fig. 9.   Austin areas of 25 percent or more black public
                         elementary school children, 1967–71. Source:
                         Center for Urban Studies, University of Chicago

The Chicago Board of Education had never pursued a vigorous policy of racial integration. This is not surprising considering the highly segregated residential pattern and hence the
formidable logistics involved, not to mention political obstacles. But racial integration was part of the new plan for
Chicago's schools proposed by Superintendent James Redmond
shortly after he took office in 1966, replacing Benjamin Willis,
who was extremely unpopular with the black community in
Chicago and had been repeatedly charged by black leaders with
consciously perpetuating school segregation. In Redmond's
plan, two neighborhoods were targeted to begin the desegregation program: the South Shore community on Chicago's
southeast side and Austin.[4]

If desegregation was to begin anywhere, Austin was not an

unlikely site. Pressure to desegregate was coming from some quarters of the Austin community itself, especially from the Organization for a Better Austin (OBA). OBA had pointed out that while southern Austin's schools were overflowing, not many blocks north there were classrooms standing unused. Some of the Chicago School Board members found themselves able to support at least voluntary busing to relieve overcrowding even when they opposed busing for the primary purpose of desegregation.[5]

It was thus that, in the fall of 1968, 573 pupils who would normally have attended May and Spencer schools were assigned to schools in northern Austin and elsewhere on the northwest side of the city. When school opened that September, the busloads of black children were met in the white, working-class destination neighborhoods by angry, placard-bearing mothers. But no serious violence occurred, and the busing program continued in subsequent years.

In 1976 some white parents and even some teachers in the receiving schools still privately expressed hostility toward the busing program. Board members, on the other hand, were calling for the Austin busing program to be expanded, since the board had received warning from the Illinois Office of Education that state aid would be terminated if the entire Chicago public school system did not desegregate. But otherwise Chicago's first school busing plan had gone largely unnoticed throughout the city, once the headlines of September 1968 had faded.

As the small scale of the busing program indicated, it was never intended as the final remedy for overcrowding in southern Austin schools. Clearly, more classrooms had to be provided in south Austin itself. The most pressing shortages of space were met by setting up "demountables" on the playgrounds of existing schools. These were prefabricated units that could be readily assembled to meet immediate needs, then taken down when they were no longer required. Ultimately the problem was in part resolved by building additional schools, including two "middle schools" for the intermediate grades. The OBA was the main local community force behind all of these Board of Education moves.

While OBA pressed its demands for new facilities to accom-
modate a changing and growing population, a rival organization, the Town Hall Assembly (THA) carried on an ultimately
fruitless campaign to return the Austin High School attendance
area boundaries to their pre-1964 location, the area to be
excluded being almost totally black. Without ever taking an
explicit position of "holding the line" against blacks in Austin,
THA was nevertheless always far more reluctant than OBA to
accept programs that implicitly recognized the reality of racial
change. Thus THA supported, though with no great enthusiasm, construction of new school buildings in southern
Austin ("where they are needed," in the words of one THA
spokesman), they opposed busing, and they opposed construction of one of the two new middle schools on a site just north of
Lake Street, which was at that time seen as the racial dividing
line. Among the reasons given for opposition were that the area
immediately surrounding the site was already too congested
and, more significantly, that additional classrooms were not
needed in northern Austin. This meant, of course, that THA
was not willing to anticipate a repetition in northern Austin of
the process of change then occurring in the southern half of the
community.

Despite OBA's claims of success in its efforts to improve the
local school situation, in the end OBA leaders came to view the
action taken by the Board of Education as too little and too late.
A former president of OBA singled out the crowded schools as
the factor that finally ended any hope of racial integration in
southern Austin. OBA and THA, which seldom agreed about
anything, were at least in unison on the importance of the
schools in the transition process, though their diagnoses and
prescriptions differed markedly.

After 1970 a pattern of school racial change was emerging in
Oak Park that was similar to the pattern in Austin in that
change in the elementary schools proceeded well ahead of racial
change in the immediate neighborhoods. But, as table 14
shows, the change was not as dramatic as in Austin, and the
very steep rises in black enrollment from one year to the next
absent. (Locations of Oak Park schools are shown in fig.
10.)

Table 14   Black Enrollments of Oak Park Public Elementary Schools, 1971–76

School	Number of Black Pupils						Percentage Black, 1976
	September 1971	October 1972	September 1973	January 1974	January 1975	June 1976	
Beye	5	9	20	22	34	59	11.4
Emerson	8	0	14	16	38	43	6.4
Hatch	1	3	12	12	25	34	6.6
Hawthorne	13	43	102	112	160	218	28.2
Holmes	7	6	7	7	12	15	3.3
Irving	0	2	9	9	18	21	3.3
Lincoln	7	7	11	11	11	14	2.1
Longfellow	19	54	71	83	113	135	14.9
Mann	1	7	14	14	15	15	2.8
Whittier	6	8	15	16	20	44	7.0

Source: Oak Park Public Schools, District 97.

Neighborhood Schools and Community Institutions

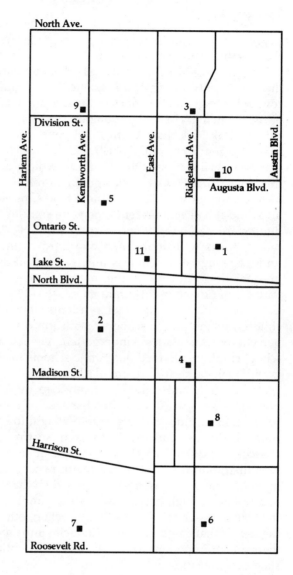

Fig. 10.   Location of Oak Park public schools

Oak Park public schools:

1. Beye
2. Emerson
3. Hatch
4. Hawthorne
5. Holmes
6. Irving
7. Lincoln
8. Longfellow
9. Mann
10. Whittier
11. High School

Although by 1975 at least two of Oak Park's elementary schools, Hawthorne and Longfellow on the southeast side, seemed in danger of "tipping," several factors worked together to prevent the school situation from being as great a liability to racial stabilization as in Austin.

First, the age structure of Oak Park's population at the time the community began to experience racial change was more conducive to gradual changes in the size and racial composition of the elementary-school population than had been the case in Austin. Oak Park, like Austin, had gone through several decades of aging; but, unlike Austin, Oak Park had seen a regeneration if its life cycle with an influx of young white families in the 1960s.[6] In 1970 Oak Park's population had a median age of 35.6, compared with 28.4 for the whole Chicago metropolitan area, and it had 16.3 percent who were sixty-five or older. Both figures are deceiving, however, since Oak Park also had four census tracts with more than one-third of their populations under age eighteen, whereas this was true of only one tract in pretransition Austin. Furthermore, although many of Oak Park's young white in-migrants of the 1960s were Roman Catholic, they, like the older residents, tended to send their children to the public schools,[7] with the result that only 26.6 percent of Oak Park's kindergarten, elementary, and high-school children attended nonpublic schools in 1970. Therefore, even if Oak Park's in-migrant blacks were similar in age, family characteristics, and school preference to those who had first moved into south Austin, the character of the existing white population would serve as a counterweight to keep the balance from shifting as suddenly as it did in Austin.

Second, the Oak Park elementary school board and the school administration were able to deal with racial change as it began to occur, instead of responding only when the black enrollment had reached a high proportion. While minority percentages in the Oak Park schools were still low, school officials anticipated the trends that could culminate in racial imbalance and—one of their most important considerations—potential violation of state desegregation rules.

In 1971 the Oak Park Board of Education formulated its "human dignity" statement, a policy paper affirming the value of cultural diversity and accepting promotion of cultural awareness as a task for the schools. Teacher workshops and other school programs devoted to this theme were launched, and recruiting of minority teachers was given priority. Though modest in substance, the human dignity statement and subsequent activities were symbolically important as a statement of intention and a representation of the stance the elementary school system was to take.

Another aspect of the early strategy involved special attention to Hawthorne and Longfellow schools, attempting to enhance their curricula and hence their attractiveness through innovative educational programs and methods, such as open classrooms. Parents commonly expressed high satisfaction with these schools, and parental involvement in school affairs was high. Hawthorne, especially, was often cited by individuals throughout the village as a prime example of good school-community relations and active parent participation.

However, the rising proportions of minority students in the east-side schools eventually called for more forceful intervention. In 1975, Hawthorne School had a minority (black, other nonwhite, and Hispanic) enrollment of 34 percent, with an even greater concentration of minority pupils in the primary grades, while Mann School in northwest Oak Park had a minority enrollment of only 6 percent. Clearly, Oak Park had fallen out of compliance with state regulations that called for the minority enrollment of any school to be within 15 percent of the minority population of the district.

The district administration began drafting alternative reorganization plans to bring the schools back into racial balance. The plan that was approved by the school board in 1976 and took effect that fall called for transformation of Hawthorne and Emerson schools into junior high schools, leaving the remaining schools as "K–6" (elementary) facilities. By reassigning Hawthorne and Emerson pupils to other schools and feeding pupils from the northeast and southwest quadrant elementary schools into Emerson and those from the northwest and southeast into Hawthorne, the school board hoped to achieve a school assignment plan that would keep the district in compliance in years to come, even if black residence continued to be concentrated on the eastern edge of Oak Park. The plan required busing of 1,555 children in the first year. Since the neighborhood school concept was retained for the kindergarten through sixth grades, there was still disparity among the elementary schools' minority enrollments. But, because of the way the junior high schools and their feeder elementary schools were matched, racial balance at these grade levels could be predicted for some years to come.

The reorganization plan was passed despite vociferous opposition from local groups and individuals. But traditional liberal and conservative labels were of little use in predicting the source and nature of the opposition and support. Opposition came from neighborhoods in which the black school enrollment would be lower than before as well as from those that would receive more black students in their schools. A school official who had met with many community groups on the issue of school reorganization described those neighborhoods south of the Eisenhower Expressway as more hostile to the plan than the rest of Oak Park. Local imagery portrayed these neighborhoods as having the deepest conservatism on racial issues and the lowest attachment to the values of the community elites.

Since there were no reliable opinion surveys, it is impossible to estimate with any accuracy how many supported or opposed the plan. However, two indirectly related ballot tests at least suggested that the action taken by the Board of Education had not undercut the legitimacy of the school leadership. In December 1976 Oak Park voters approved bond issues for both the elementary and the high schools, entailing an overall tax increase of 11 percent. Then in the elementary school board elections the following spring candidates endorsed by the influential Parent-Teacher Organization as usual claimed all the seats, soundly defeating their opposition. Neither of these events suggest a deeply alienated constituency.

Many of the busing opponents accused the school administration of using children as pawns to achieve racial balance that ought instead to be pursued through open housing. On the other hand, there were also those who favored busing precisely because they thought it would help prevent neighborhood resegregation in eastern Oak Park. Yet both these arguments were somewhat beside the point. In fact, school officials initiated early action, beginning with the human dignity policy, because they foresaw a time when the district would be in violation of the law, and they instituted busing when that prediction came true.

The high school board, in contrast, was often criticized by local leaders for lagging behind the elementary schools in race relations. But the high school, which served both River Forest and Oak Park, had only a 5.3 percent black enrollment even in 1976, and in any case could never be out of compliance with integration rules, since there was only one school in the district. The motivation that impelled elementary school officials was lacking.

The schools constituted an institutional sector of the community with their own rules, roles, resources, and motives providing the normative structure within which their officials had to act. This is not to assert that the schools were free from outside political pressures. For example, the school board may have been able to take early and strong action only because those policies were supported by a well-entrenched community elite as well as a substantial share of the citizenry at large, who saw neighborhood racial stability as the ultimate goal. But the school board would have been stepping beyond its limits of legitimacy had it also adopted this as the aim of the busing program.

Nevertheless, busing did aid the community's effort to achieve residential integration by at least forestalling racial tipping in east Oak Park schools. This illustrates a pattern which we have already seen in our discussion of the real estate industry and which we shall see repeated in later discussions of other Oak Park organizations and institutions. That is, institutions operating from divergent motives and within quite different constraints developed objectives and tactics that led to a convergence of results. This pattern resulted in a sort of "layering" and overlapping of actions and effects in different quarters of the community, and it contributed greatly to the strength of Oak Park's overall integration effort.

Of course the Chicago Board of Education was under even more pressure to desegregate than was Oak Park's board, having been explicitly threatened with loss of state aid. But the Chicago system was enormous and already highly segregated, and the majority of its students were nonwhite or Hispanic. Its inability to desegregate the entire system of elementary and high schools was not difficult to understand, and to expect it to take action that would aid neighborhood integration specifically in Austin would have been altogether unrealistic. Racial change in Austin's schools was merely a repetition of a pattern that had been occurring all over the city for many years. The Chicago Board of Education, taxed with many problems in its many schools, could at best apply the palliatives of altered attendance boundaries, permissive transfers, and the like.

By contrast, in Oak Park the school board was dealing with a much more manageable system. Furthermore, it was a local system, with boundaries coinciding with those of the village, so that its only constituency was the Oak Park community. It was an elected board, unlike Chicago's appointed body, and thus was subject to very direct and immediate pressure to maintain quality. Its early efforts to maintain racial balance by improving the quality of the southeast side schools may partly explain why Oak Parkers did not inevitably link rising black enrollment with declining academic standards. In any case, general satisfaction with the schools was the rule, regardless of racial composition. The reputation of Oak Park schools proved an asset in the effort to achieve residential racial stability, whereas in Austin the public schools were a major liability in that fight.

Transition in Shopping Areas

Increasing black population naturally brought more black patrons to the neighborhood stores, but transition in the shopping areas was not simply the effect of residential turnover. The phenomena were intertwined.

For whites using the shopping areas, racially shifting patronage had two disturbing aspects: greater visibility of black people in the neighborhood and loss of amenities the whites had come to enjoy. Commercial transition involved at least a perceived loss of business establishments to the white community and at least a temporary loss to both blacks and whites during the transition process.

Shopping areas in Austin's transitional areas eventually shifted from all-white to all-black use in three loosely defined and overlapping stages: increasing patronage by blacks, adaptation of existing stores to increasing black patronage, and replacement of white-oriented by black-oriented establishments. Furthermore, with the exception of such relatively impermeable barriers as railroad tracks, the expressway, and large industries, shopping strips became the main perceptual markers dividing white from black neighborhoods.

Austin's first instance of commercial transition, Cicero Avenue, was also one of the most striking in the eyes of white Austinites, since many of them considered Cicero the eastern boundary of the whole community, separating it from the black west side.

Along Cicero Avenue, particularly between Lake Street and the Eisenhower Expressway, was a strip of small stores and businesses and quite a few neighborhood taverns. As more black people were seen on the street, white patronage declined. Transition from white to black occurred rapidly on Cicero Avenue, as many establishments changed ownership, others were closed and boarded up, and many were replaced by even more marginal enterprises. Street life intensified, particularly at night, as small groups of black teenagers and young adults gathered on street corners and in front of grocery stores, restaurants, and taverns. Some places became known as hangouts for street gangs. By 1966 whites still made necessary work or business trips to the area but were rarely seen there at night. Cicero gained a reputation as a dangerous, vice-ridden street, probably reinforcing the white perception of the near impenetrability of this boundary. It was the first and one of the most sharply perceived of the series of racial dividing lines that rose and fell in Austin.

Increased black patronage of a business or shopping area was one of the first triggers of real anxiety for many whites. Because commercial districts, even minor ones, drew customers from some distance away, they afforded many white people their first perceptions of the actual entrance of black people into their own daily round. As early as 1973, black pedestrians were

often in the majority along the eastern end of Madison Street in
Oak Park, although the surrounding Oak Park neighborhood
was predominantly white. The Austin neighborhood across the
street, however, was solidly black. Even in downtown Oak
Park, geographically remote from the ghetto but easily accessi-
ble by el, counts taken at the busy Lake-Marion intersection on
three summer Saturdays in 1973 revealed that blacks accounted
for as many as a quarter of the shoppers during any given time,
although on weekdays few blacks were seen there. An Oak Park
community relations staff member admitted that the numbers
of black shoppers were a source of some worry:

> The shopping district is the greatest concern to people.
> They're not used to it. They're used to going shopping and
> having it be all white. We can't really tell them that they
> don't all live here. On the other hand, we don't want to say
> that none of them live here. White people go out to the shop-
> ping centers. Black people ride the el to Oak Park. A lot of
> people from Austin shopped in Oak Park when Austin was
> still all white. It's just that blacks are so visible.

The next discernible stage was the orientation of existing
businesses to black consumer demands. Food stores seemed
especially flexible in making this adaptation. Black-oriented
food products began to be stocked and often advertised by
window posters. This happened almost routinely in Austin's
changing areas. When a large chain store that had carried a
wide selection of Chianti wine cut its stock down to one brand
and increased its selection of "pop wines" instead, even a
stranger might have guessed the nature of the ethnic shift taking place in the neighborhood.

As Molotch noted in South Shore,[8] there was practically no
mixing of blacks and whites in taverns in Austin. Blacks did go
into white taverns to buy package liquor, cigarettes, and so
forth. In at least three combination liquor store–taprooms, the
package business became predominantly black while the bar
remained white. As a rule, whites did not patronize black bars,
and in white bars only occasional black customers were to be
seen.

The established restaurants were patronized by blacks, but they usually remained predominantly white for as long as they remained in business. As white clientele dropped off, they often stayed open shorter hours before closing completely. The white bars and restaurants were victims of a temporal ecological pattern Molotch called "Saturday night segregation": a tendency toward increased racial separation at night, especially on weekends, and increased ratios of blacks to whites on the streets at night.[9] Carry-out places, especially "neutral" franchises, switched from white to black patronage more or less readily, serving a mixed clientele in the interim.

White taverns and restaurants eventually closed, and even the small shops that tried to adapt often either closed or transferred to black management. Generally speaking, the most adaptable stores were those in which the relations among customers and between clientele and store personnel were most fleeting and impersonal.

Beginning about 1973, Oak Park experienced similar changes at the eastern ends of the Madison Street, Lake Street, and Chicago Avenue commercial strips. There passersby might readily observe some of the most visible symbols of change. Posters in grocery store windows advertised chitterlings and announced that food stamps were accepted. Complaints by whites that one large food chain had begun to "cater to blacks from Austin" were numerous enough to lead to explicit public assurances (in the local newspaper) from the manager that the store would not direct its marketing primarily to the black community. Black cosmetics appeared in the drugstores. Laundromats shifted from white to black use, and patronage by either race dropped off at night. Restaurants closed early. By 1975 a few black entrepreneurs operated businesses in eastern Oak Park, but almost all shops catered to a racially mixed clientele, the notable exceptions being, as usual, the barbers and hairdressers.

As businesses in Austin closed and were replaced, the distribution of business types changed. Stores oriented to white ethnic groups predictably moved out. For example, a Gaelic import store and a restaurant specializing in British cooking left

Chicago Avenue to follow the Irish migration to the northwest side of the city. Resale and secondhand stores became more numerous on Austin's Chicago Avenue. So did short-order and carry-out restaurants. Marginal businesses proliferated, and the small buildings often experienced a succession of shops in a relatively short time. However, the large food and drug chains did not abandon Austin, and some even expanded their operations there.

The size of the average commercial structure played an important role in the fate of transitional commercial streets in Austin. Madison Street's large stores were closed and boarded up, leaving that wide thoroughfare desolated for several years. Only very slowly did it again take on any appearance of life, and it never matched its pretransition vitality. On the other hand, the small shops along Lake Street and Chicago Avenue change from white to black with little interruption.

As orderly as the transition of such business streets as Chicago Avenue was, it was not comfortable for those who lived it, white oldtimers and black newcomers alike. Trust waned, and concern for security increased. Iron bars and gates went up over doors and windows. Police records verified the perceived rise in crime. Fire was still another fear, as commercial buildings burned with what neighbors saw as suspicious frequency. Rumors, seldom confirmed or disconfirmed, of "torch jobs" abounded.

As the old understandings that governed the use of shared public space failed to adequately regulate its use by two distinct and socially distant groups, new norms emerged to introduce interim order. At best these were ad hoc adjustments that fell short of providing for mutual trust, individual peace of mind, and a sense of stability in one's everyday environment. It is hardly surprising that they failed, if only because the neighborhood was perceived as transitional, and thus the accommodations as temporary, the new norms as not to be taken for granted, and the new tacit contract as not entirely or permanently binding.

The tenuous state of race relations in Austin's transitional shopping areas was illustrated by the conversation of a white manager of a resale store with his black clerk:

I got two old white women coming in here who are giving
me trouble. They go in the back there and watch what those
[black] teenage boys are doing. If they don't see me they'll
say something to the boys. Well, you don't do that. One time
one of them threw a plate at the woman. Another time, one of
the boys came in here and said to me, "Who told you I stole
this? She told you, didn't she?" I said to her, "Listen, you
leave those boys alone. They'll get to your house before you
do and then you'll really have troubles." If she goes stirring
up things, I'm apt to get my windows broken. But I've been
good to them all winter, so I hope they'll leave me alone this
summer. I give 'em baseball gloves—hell, those things sell
for fifty cents apiece. Trouble is, I got 'em spoiled. They come
in here and they always want something for free. The idea is,
this is the last day of school, and I don't want them coming in
here every day, every day.

Of course, it was not only the white residents who experienced such trials of transition. In a neighborhood white residents perceived as being "taken over" by black people, the
black newcomers were just as mindful as the whites of the new
unwritten rules of interaction and the territorial bounds that
separated the races, and they traveled the interstices of shared
space, such as Chicago Avenue, with just as much trepidation.
One black woman, for example, noted that the white neighborhood north of Chicago Avenue was so tough that blacks could
not even cross that street to shop in a major supermarket on its
north side. She was partly mistaken, for black shoppers were at
that time much in evidence in the store, but the neighborhood
was indeed reputed to be tough, and her fears, if not entirely
justified, were real enough.

Community
Institutions

Organizations other than commercial ones felt the effect of racial change. Many of Austin's churches were sold as their old
congregations moved away. Others tried to adapt to a changing
constituency.

An example of the latter was Saint Thomas Aquinas Roman Catholic Church in southeast Austin. At its peak in the 1940s and 1950s, it had served between two and three thousand families. In 1972 it had fewer than four hundred families on its rolls, and few of these were white. The order of nuns who had taught at the parish school left. However, the priests were active in local community organizations and were committed to serving the needs of the neighborhood. For example, the "soul-patrol," a two-way radio network that permitted quick contact with the police, had its headquarters in the church basement.

The Catholic churches in Austin had been accustomed to direct involvement in secular, neighborhood affairs. The changing racial composition of the neighborhood did not change this inclination. Furthermore, Catholic churches are more likely than Protestant churches to have their constituencies defined by geography rather than by voluntary membership. The Catholic churches changed from white to black, though with drastically reduced memberships, but the Protestant churches usually just dwindled and died or moved away. A very notable exception in south Austin was the Third Unitarian Church, whose predominantly politically liberal white congregation determined to stay and was still there in 1977, though the surrounding neighborhood was virtually all black.

An Episcopal church in southern Austin was left with only a dozen worshipers by August 1973 when it finally closed, and only one of those still lived in Austin. The large old Methodist church across from the Town Hall was sold to a black congregation, as were other white churches, a synagogue, the Knute Rockne VFW Post, a white funeral home, and a number of houses and storefronts.

Such community institutions, oriented toward the primary end of the scale of social relations, did not feel the same pressure in Oak Park. The black population there was still too small. Nor did black institutions and organizations arise alongside the white ones in Oak Park. One black resident speculated that blacks moving into Oak Park from Chicago might prefer to maintain social and personal ties in their former communities:

one of the attractions of Oak Park was that its proximity to the city allowed this.

In contrast, the experience of Austin's Town Hall area provides a microcosmic and highly significant view of what was happening throughout that community. This area was of great symbolic significance and had always been viewed by Austinites as the "heart" of Austin. Saint Lucy Roman Catholic Church, serving that area, lost three-fourths of its parishioners between 1960 and 1973. In 1973 it closed its grammar school, sending its pupils to Saint Catherine of Siena on the Oak Park–Austin border, a school that had already become almost 50 percent black. Finally the parish itself merged with Saint Catherine, an exception to the rule that the Roman Catholic churches remained in the changed neighborhoods. Of course the former Saint Lucy parish continued to be served by the combined parishes.

Many commercial establishments fled the Town Hall area and were replaced by shops catering to black patrons. Much of the land immediately surrounding the Town Hall was either vacant or occupied by abandoned and dilapidated buildings, the result of an aborted urban renewal project. The new public school nearby had been opposed by many of the neighborhood's white residents, who feared it would bring more black children into the neighborhood. When it opened in 1973 it was already 97 percent black.

As fewer and fewer of the visible symbols of white dominance remained, whites said that Austin had "gone down the drain." They spoke, of course, from an extremely limited perspective, but it was the only one that mattered to them. Indeed, their community had vanished. A new community was being forged in the black block clubs, churches, businesses, and community organizations.

7

Perceptions of Race and Community

It should be clear that actual events associated with racial change and people's perceptions of those events are not identical. The events and the perceptions interact in a continuous process of mutual modification or reinforcement. So far I have attempted to focus primarily on the nature of the events themselves, though it has not been possible to do so without bringing up perceptual matters. In this chapter attention shifts to the nature of the perceptions of race and community and to the related issue of the social construction and reconstruction of the communities in the context of racial change.

Strictly speaking, perceiving is done by individuals, and when we speak of perceptions by groups of people we are using a kind of shorthand. Individual perceptions pass back and forth through channels of communication, which filter and catalyze them, giving rise to shared bodies of knowledge and belief. The community is socially constructed in a continuous and dynamic process that involves the interplay of individual perceptions, shared knowledge and beliefs, and the definitions formulated by local leaders and institutions. This process shapes the image, identity, and sense of integrity of the community as seen by residents and outsiders.[1] The resulting representation of community has been viewed as very largely a product of the activities of the local elites. As long as residents' felt needs are being adequately met, the running and representation of the community can be left to the custodial care of the local elite; that is, the leaders of political, business, religious, and voluntary organizations, the local press, and so forth. Racial change profoundly alters the situation, however, provoking new perceptions and making it necesssary to redefine the community. In this unbalanced state of altered events, changing perceptions, and redefining of the situation, the mutual interdependence of all these aspects becomes very important.

Residents' Perceptions of Racial Change

The entry of even a few blacks into a previously all-white community is seldom seen by white residents as a casual event. In Austin and Oak Park, adjacent to a heavily black residential area, it had a profound effect on the way the communities came to be perceived by local residents and outsiders alike. Many comments and observations made in the course of ordinary everyday conversation alluded to and reflected the people's perceptions of racial change and the perceived effect of that change on the communities. For example, a teacher at an Austin school encountered a former student and, upon learning that the student had moved to an Oak Park neighborhood near Austin Boulevard, said, "You'll be moving soon, won't you?" Although race had not been mentioned, the former student responded quite appropriately, "No, I think it will be all right for a while yet. There is only one black family on the block."

An Oak Park dentist, when informed that one of his Austin patients was moving away, said, "I guess a lot of people will be leaving. I think they're silly, myself." Again, race was not mentioned, but was understood. The following conversation took place one evening as I visited friends on the western edge of Oak Park. One woman, learning that I lived in the eastern part of the community, volunteered that a friend of hers had lived nearby, "over on the other side of West Suburban Hospital for twenty-seven years, and she had to move." Since the block to which she referred had not experienced a great many black move-ins at that time, I said, "I'm surprised. I know that on the Austin side..." but before I could finish she interjected, "Oh, Austin is black." I replied, "I know, but the Oak Park side is still pretty white." She looked at me skeptically, then said with an air of assurance and finality, "Well, they were in her building."

During a conversation between an Oak Park woman and a woman who lived in Chicago not far north of Oak Park, a certain western suburb was mentioned. The Chicago woman replied, "Oh, this man I know at work lives there. He used to live in Oak Park. He lived in Oak Park for years, but then he moved out there. I don't know why. Maybe he lived over by Austin."

Other comments were grounded in similar assumptions, and they revealed a variety of dimensions of the perception of race and community:

Oak Park will be in exactly the same situation that Austin is in now in three to five years.

North Oak Park will probably hold. South Oak Park looks just like Austin.

We're going to change. We're either going up or going down. We're either going to be an Austin or we're going to develop.... We can either change or we can stay the same and be like Austin.... Oak Park is not going to become another Austin.

Let's not be an ostrich and put your head in the sand. Oak Park has been deteriorating. I've been here sixteen or seventeen years, and Oak Park's not what it used to be. Let's not hide ourselves. Let's face it: many people here probably have their homes up for sale.... It's a big secret now who's selling.

I take my son to hockey games out in the western suburbs, and as soon as people find out we're from Oak Park, they say, "Gee, I hear that's going black."

These illustrations reveal certain perceptual dimensions of community identity in the context of racial change. First, the salience of the prospect or fact of racial change was indicated by the way it was often taken for granted in casual conversation. It existed at a cognitive level that might be characterized as "everybody knows." It was possible and even usual to talk about the predicted or feared effects of changing community racial composition without ever making explicit mention of race, which was clearly unnecessary for mutual understanding.

Reference to race was not the only thing customarily omitted from the explicit level of the conversation. There frequently were unstated but mutually understood assumptions. For example, it was taken for granted that black in-migration was an understandable motive for white out-migration, even when it was not approved. The phrase "had to move" needed no explication for either integrationists or exclusionists, though they might disagree radically over the validity of its implications. Place names also became code words for processes. The phrase "southeast Oak Park" did more than locate an area geographically. "What happened in Austin" had a meaning to Oak Parkers that they might find difficult to explicate fully, but its referent was unquestionable. Race was an extremely salient issue, but discussion of it was also highly elliptical. Even when it was not mentioned, it was no less surely part of the shared world view in which context judgments, intentions, and observations had their full meanings.

Another point is that the communities acquired stigmatized identities among whites at a very early stage in the invasion-succession process. Early in 1977, after Oak Park had received extremely favorable publicity in national newspapers and magazines as well as in the Chicago metropolitan press and had been the subject of at least three local television specials, an Oak Park real estate broker observed that Oak Park was just beginning to see the effects of such positive exposure. He said that attitudes of whites outside Oak Park were "just beginning to turn around." My own observations and experiences confirm that Oak Park was still viewed by many who lived in other parts of the Chicago area as a "changing neighborhood."

Whereas community leaders and residents of changing areas attempted to minimize the extent of change at its earliest stages, residents of other areas were prone to exaggerate the presence of blacks. The north Oak Parker's statement that south Oak Park looked "just like Austin," made at a time when south Oak Park had a black population of well under one thousand and Austin's black population was many times that, was understandable and even valid if taken as subjective evaluation rather than objective description. Such descriptions-cum-evaluations were oriented to individual needs, interests, and goals. Minimizing the extent of racial change was psychologically functional for those who had a stake in the neighborhood. It supported residents' attachments to the neighborhood and was congruent with their desire not to move. It reduced the dissonance between their negative evaluations of black neighbors and their other positive evaluations of the local neighborhood. The converse of this was the exaggeration of racial change by outsiders. This was rooted in the functions of the "cognitive maps" with which individuals organize geographic space and imbue it with social meaning. The cognitive maps constructed for the portions of space other than that which individuals are bound to occupy or traverse regularly—local neighborhoods, the paths to and from places of work and other routine activities, etc.—are likely to be no more refined than is necessary to make certain crucial distinctions: safe from unsafe areas, high-status from low-status areas, and so forth.[2] Especially in the urban setting, there is so much space to be organized that the details of the maps must be left out. Hence "black" is not qualified by numbers or proportions but simply signals to whites, "stay away."

This can be illustrated by some additional examples. For instance, a north suburbanite was surprised to hear that Austin was still 50 percent white in 1973. "But it doesn't have that reputation," he said. "People think of it as black."

Both the minimizing of race by the local resident and its exaggeration by the outsider are illustrated in one short exchange between an Oak Park resident and a man from another western suburb. The man asked, "It's getting pretty black in Oak Park, isn't it?" The Oak Parker replied, "No, there are only about twelve hundred blacks." "Jesus!" the man responded, "That's a lot!"

Another device used by residents of changing neighborhoods to reduce their own cognitive dissonance and enhance the image of the community was to emphasize the high social status of in-migrant blacks. For example, an Oak Park businessman commented: "I consider myself fortunate enough to have a minority family on my block. This man has a gardener working for him. Why, I can't even afford to have a gardener. My kids are my gardeners."

In both Austin and Oak Park, residents often called attention to the positive qualities of their black neighbors—qualities that would have been taken for granted had they been white.

The presence of even a small number of blacks in a neighborhood where racial change is anticipated seems to become a dominant feature, a characteristic analogous to what we call a "master status trait" in an individual. The master status trait connotes the presence of a collection of additional traits that are objectively unrelated.[3] It defines one's identity to others. Black residents in a community and black skin color in individuals, though representing different levels of organization, come to be very similar social stigmata.

Whatever else may be said about the perception and meaning of black residential in-migration, the most common and generally undeniable element is a basic negative evaluation of the event by white residents. This is especially true if substantial numbers of black people are involved.

The white aversion to sharing residential space with black neighbors is, we can guess, deeply rooted in such basic things as feelings of discomfort associated with social distance, protection of primary-group life from elements perceived to be discordant, display of prestige through home and neighborhood, internalized fears and prejudices, and other psychological and social psychological phenomena; but, however deep and disguised the actual roots of the prejudice are, white residents are seldom slow to present their own explanations. These often come in the form of racial stereotypes, and imputing deviant, particularly criminal, behavior to black people is one of the most common examples.

Fear of crime and fear of declining property values were two of the most frequent objections to black in-migration voiced by white residents of Austin and Oak Park. Of the two, fear of crime was easily the leader. It was the most frequently heard reason for leaving or avoiding a racially changing neighborhood.

The fear was partly justified by rising crime rates in both Austin and Oak Park. Since the middle of the 1960s, crime in Austin had steadily escalated. During the first five months of 1973, the Austin police district had thirty-five murders, more than any other district in the city.

Crime was the most disturbing issue for Oak Parkers, too, since they were well aware of the dramatic increases in Austin's crime rate. In 1971 Oak Park's crime rate was up only 6 percent over the preceding year. In 1972 it rose another 8 percent. But robberies had tripled over a three-year period, and this type of crime caused particular anxiety because it involved personal contact with the criminal and the potential for bodily harm.

More important than police statistics, however, was the rising perception of crime and personal danger, which residents linked with racial change. Although residents' perception of increased danger was consistent with police statistics, it had sources that were not dependent on official reports or linked perfectly to actual levels of crime. Instead, the perception of the danger of crime built up gradually as individuals received information from a variety of channels and from personal experience and interpreted this information in accordance with their own prior beliefs and motivations.

Expectedly, the greatest anxiety was in the areas nearest the site of ghetto expansion. The largest number of crimes were, in fact, reported in these areas; but, for Oak Park especially, the level of anxiety seemed higher than the level of actual danger.

Residents of one Austin neighborhood hired a private security patrol. Residents of southeast Oak Park considered doing the same, but they abandoned the plan when local police promised extra patrols. "Operation Whistlestop" campaigns were put into effect in fringe neighborhoods of both Austin and Oak Park. Residents carried whistles to blow when they witnessed any suspicious activity. This was to serve as a signal for others to call the police and as a deterrent to the criminal.

One Austin resident noted that Chicago Avenue was virtually abandoned by whites at night, because they feared to go out. An Oak Parker living a block away from Austin Boulevard said that the women who came to her house for club meetings, even in the daytime, carried nothing but the necessities and kept little money in their purses. A professional woman who lived in an apartment on Austin Boulevard was thinking of moving because, she said, "I wouldn't exactly say I am living in fear, but I am afraid much of the time." Comments such as these are but fragmentary samplings of the frequently expressed feelings of residents of the transitional or fringe neighborhoods in Austin and Oak Park during 1972 and 1973.

In the context of neighborhood racial change, white fear of crime takes on a unique quality. Part of this quality is an added intensity, often seemingly unwarranted by reality. A threat is felt beyond the natural fear of bodily harm. Because the fear of injury is so natural and gripping, perception of interpersonal crime in changing neighborhoods readily serves as a cover for a multitude of other unexpressed fears. Personal danger may not be the sole or even the main fear of white residents, but it is capable of summarizing and encapsulating many dimensions of threat associated with neighborhood change, and it seems rational and socially acceptable. As we have already seen, the language of racial change is one of code words and ellipses. This is especially well illustrated by the issue of crime. It is the combination of threats that crime both embodies and symbolizes that makes fear of crime so overwhelming for whites in transitional areas.

Crime and the Outsider Theory

In the context of racial change, crime is perceived not only as a violation of personal space, but also as a violation of community space, lending it a double impact. By violation of community space I mean, first, that crime is often carefully attributed to "outsiders"—people coming from outside the territorial bounds of the community. It is perceived as a part of a general external assault on the community carried on by real estate brokers, city and federal governments, and so forth. However, the territorial aspect is important primarily in that it spatially defines an assumed community of shared norms and values.

The concept of community implies both territorial and normative integrity. That crime was seen as a violation of the territorial rights of the communities was illustrated by the pains community leaders and representatives took to link crimes to nonresident offenders. It became very important to connect crime to outsiders.

In the early stages of change in Austin, the *Austinite* frequently attributed increased street crime to outsiders (black was understood) who patronized the Cicero Avenue strip of "honky-tonks" and "dives" or who were lured there by their perceptions of criminal opportunity. The clear implication that was carefully tendered was that the offenders were not Austin's own black residents, who were assumed to be upright and law-abiding citizens sharing the norms of the white Austinites.

Oak Park leaders were equally impelled to attribute crime to outsiders. The police chief stated: "I would estimate that 90 percent of serious crime in Oak Park is committed by individuals from outside the village.... I recently questioned a purse snatcher and asked him why he came to Oak Park from Chicago. He said it was because 'there was no bread [money] in Chicago.'"[4]

It was generally understood by Oak Parkers that the outsiders who committed crimes in their village were blacks from Austin. Likewise, the common explanation of increasing crime in Oak Park was the transition of southern Austin from white to black. On one occasion, however, the police chief placed the source of the threat even farther away. When asked if he noticed a correlation between transition in Austin and crime in Oak Park, he replied that this seemed to be less a factor than the opening of the Dan Ryan rapid transit line, which linked Oak Park with Chicago's far south side. His perception may have been accurate; but it does not seem to stretch the point to suggest that the claim served another function. The fate of Oak Park was clearly associated with that of Austin. An outsider from Austin might still be uncomfortably close. Furthermore, Austin blacks had legitimate roles in the Oak Park community—for example, as shoppers or churchgoers. It was convenient to trust, at least minimally, blacks who came into the village for such purposes, just as it was necessary to foster some level of trust in the black residents of the village.

The outsider theory, which applies not only in crime but also to other agencies and individuals with which the local community faced with racial change has inimical or problematic dealings, functions to give the community the appearance of a solid front, undivided in its response to crisis.

But at some point in the process of transition incidents occur that cannot be explained away by the outsider theory. Then internal racial conflict becomes an inescapable problem. In Austin fighting among children and their petty crimes often most disturbed white residents.

The matter took a somewhat different twist in Oak Park. When plainly internal conflict took place, deviance was sometimes attributed not to outsiders, but to newcomers not socialized to the community culture. Occasionally there were instances of harassment of black residents or assaults on black teenagers by white youths. In these cases, Oak Parkers tended to identify the troublemakers as people who had recently fled transition in Austin to find refuge in Oak Park. For example, an Oak Park community relations official had this to say about a fight between black and white students at the high school: "There were some boys there who were previously from Austin, and they thought they knew the way to stabilize Oak Park was to beat up all the blacks . . . . Some of our people got the idea that prejudice in Oak Park is all imported, that we don't have any of our own. This is baloney, of course. There's prejudice everywhere."

The Violation of
Community Norms

This territorial aspect has a symbolic significance in that territorial boundaries spatially define a community of what are presumed to be shared norms and values. That crime violates societal or legal norms becomes less important than the feeling that "they live differently than we do" and that the cultural space of the community has been violated. Attitudes toward crime become just another dimension of a perceived value conflict between the resident in-group and the potentially in-migrant out-group. "Legal" and "illegal" are not the relevant categories; local community values are.

This was evidenced in the way white residents of Austin and Oak Park frequently lumped together crime and other undesirable, though legal, behavior in their casual references to the issue. A speaker at a local neighborhood meeting put the matter plainly:

> Basically what we're talking about is the poor and the rich, rather than anything to do with race. It happens that most of the Negroes tend to be poor, and that most of the poor tend to be Negroes, so when we see one we say, "here is a poor Negro." . . . The poor cannot pay taxes. They cannot maintain their homes, whatever you want to call that—disrepair— which gives a bad impression when anybody drives through the town looking for a house and declines the property values of all the homes in the area. They do not—and this is an absolute, proven fact—the poor do not, they cannot, they're not motivated to join community organizations, groups, contribute in any way, regardless of the amount of money or time they might have. So we can call them asocial—not necessarily anti-, but certainly not concerned with their community, and they have a very strong drive to be criminal.[5]

Crime tended to be seen as part of a constellation of undesirable attributes of black people, and these tended to be conceptualized and expressed as a "package." The speaker quoted above happened to be a social scientist, as well as a resident of Oak Park. But the view he espoused was not so different from that expressed in different words by average residents. The following remarks by an Austin woman were extreme in their vehemence, but not so atypical in the underlying beliefs they expressed; and although the social scientist's distinction between class and race escaped this woman, notice how similar the content is:

> I don't want to move, but I have to. They're coming
> like flies—the colored. I can't stand them. They go down the
> street with those big hairdos. They make so much noise with
> that music and their motorcycles and loud cars. They always
> have that loud music going. They have a tendency to steal
> and to kill. They'll shoot you, or they'll stab you. The better
> ones don't want to live with them. They say, "They'll steal
> your eyes out. They'll steal your eyes out." I wouldn't mind
> them even living next door if they lived decent, if they were
> morally clean and physically clean. And they're always
> laughing. They say they're poor, but they're the happiest
> poor people I've ever seen. Really. Did you ever see a colored
> person who wasn't always happy?

But at least some white people who stayed on in the fringe neighborhoods gradually realized that at least some of their fears were baseless and, for what it was worth, learned to separate real from imagined hazards. An Oak Park woman was telling her companions of an incident involving a "big black man" who, it seemed, had come to her door selling something and had gone away without incident when she turned him down. But she described the occurrence at great length and with considerable agitation, recalling how frightened she had been. As she built toward what was by this time obviously to be an anticlimax, one of the friends facetiously supplied the missing dramatic denouement by interjecting, "And then he killed you!" This brought laughter from all but the narrator, who seemed bewildered that her friends did not realize the seriousness of the matter.

Sources of Perceptions
of Crime

If, as suggested above, the belief that an area is becoming dangerous is imperfectly linked to "facts" such as official statistics or firsthand knowledge of specific crimes, how is the belief fostered and transmitted? Clearly, it is learned and transmitted through the routine channels of communication: informal word of mouth, the journalistic media, literature circulated by community groups, and so forth.

In the two communities, word of mouth was most frequently alluded to as the source of beliefs that particular areas might be especially dangerous. The police, much to the chagrin of police department officials, were also a source of some of the rumors of crime waves or increasing danger. For instance, one woman became worried only after being stopped on the street one night by an officer in a patrol car who asked her, "What are you doing out? You shouldn't be here." The police chief, when informed about this incident, treated it as a joke that had unfortunately been taken seriously. Another Oak Park resident reported:

> Right after we moved in here a few months ago, there was a burglary in our building, and we asked the policeman if there was much crime in the neighborhood. He said, "No," that it was unusual. Then just a couple of weeks ago, a friend of mine was attacked right up here on Iowa Street. The policeman told her that this was a high-crime area. So in just a few months this has gone from an area with not much crime to a high-crime area.

The police in these instances were probably taken more seriously because of the expert status attributed to them. It would be a mistake, however, to make too much of this expert status, for the police chief himself, even armed with statistics, had a difficult time persuading residents that Oak Park's crime increases were not out of line with those experienced by many other suburbs. It is more likely that the nature of the message and its relation to existing beliefs and motivations was most important. Information on crime was sufficiently varied and ambiguous to allow selective perception and assimilation of bits of information.

Personal experience was, of course, important for those who did become victims, but these were obviously in the minority. The ever-present "friend" or "friend of a friend" was a potent

source of information in the absence of firsthand experience.
Even then, the information was often vague and not related to
specific incidents. One new resident of Oak Park pointed to a
building on Austin Boulevard, saying:

> We looked at an apartment there when we were looking for a
> place in Oak Park. We decided that we definitely did not
> want to live across from Columbus Park. A guy my room-
> mate went to school with lives down here, and he says it's
> really getting bad. It wasn't so bad about a year ago when he
> moved here, but apparently it's got worse since April. It
> seems that lately there has been a rash of purse snatchings
> and robberies and assaults and rapes and those nice things.

Newspaper reports were also sources of information about
the prevalence of crime, but people mentioned them less frequently than they did personal anecdotes. One person said, "If
you want to know the things that are going on around here, just
read the *Economist*." The *Economist* was an Oak Park weekly
newspaper that, at the time, was frequently criticized by community leaders for its prominent coverage of local crime. But
in many cases information acquired from the press was simply
used to support beliefs already held. When a metropolitan daily
paper published a list of crime statistics for the suburbs,
showing an increase in Oak Park, a resident said, "Did you see
yesterday's *Chicago Today*? That just confirms what we've been
saying."

Managing Perceptions
of Crime

Despite the apparently limited effect of published sources on
the perception of crime, newspapers often came under attack
for printing allegedly inflammatory stories. The Oak Park
Economist was particularly criticized for disproportionate attention to crime news and for printing the race of the offender,
which none of the other three community papers did. However,
one black man said he was glad the *Economist* had that policy,
because otherwise whites would probably assume all the crimi-
nals were black.

It seemed that for those involved with the racial stabilization of the communities, news media were the least acceptable sources of information about crime. These people did not seem to object to word-of-mouth circulation of information, as long as it did not reach exaggerated proportions. In fact, they manipulated the fear of crime for their own organizational ends—for example, to arouse people to become involved or to support demands for better police protection. A community leader who protested the *Economist's* coverage of crime in a letter to its editor nevertheless circulated in his neighborhood a flier headed "Oak Park Citizens against Crime," with the following text:

> Citizens are becoming concerned about the rash of petty crimes on the increase in our neighborhood—burglaries—purse snatchings—beatings—etc.
> We refuse to be driven out of our homes and we believe something can be done to correct this situation.
> By working together we are going to make our area safe.

The same man told a skeptic, who said she did not feel particularly unsafe in the neighborhood, about several assaults and burglaries within a two-block radius.

Similarly, Oak Park Citizens' Action Program, a frequent critic of newspaper handling of crime news, distributed a flier headed "Crime" in inch-high thick black letters. The text outlined selected crime statistics, including a robbery rate in 1972 that was fifteen times higher than the 1964–66 rate for Oak Park and more than triple the suburban average. The literature disseminated by community groups in both Austin and Oak Park sometimes seemed more "inflammatory" than what they criticized so severely in the local press.

The objections to press handling of crime news were rooted in the indiscriminate and uncontrollable nature of the media: that is, they were indiscriminate in their audience and the effects were beyond the control of the local leaders and community organizations. On the one hand, crime news stories reached those who were habitually uninvolved in civic affairs. Such

people were not likely to attend meetings or to have contact
with civic leaders, and their perceptions could not be appropriately molded to motivate them to the desired community participation. Apathetic residents were always a worry to community leaders, for the situation was one to which Kornhauser's
conclusions about community referenda apply: Citizens who
are least integrated into the community power structure ultimately cast the deciding "votes" on the issue.[6] Those residents least connected with the normal power and influence
networks were the ones most beyond the control of those networks. All the strategies of education and management of
perceptions did not reach them. They could cast the deciding "vote" on the issue simply by withdrawing from the
community.

News stories of crime also reached another important audience that was beyond the control of local leaders: residents of
other communities. Therefore the stories could adversely affect
the community image as it was perceived by a wider metropolitan reference group—most crucially, the market for new
white residents. This would account for the Oak Park leaders'
continually high level of concern over stories printed in the
Trib, a three-times-a-week supplement distributed to many
western suburbs inside the *Chicago Tribune*. On one occasion a
few hundred residents pooled funds to buy a full-page advertisement in the paper, protesting a story it had run about Oak
Park under the headline, "Fear Stalks the Streets in Changing
Neighborhood." The *Trib* story was common talk around Oak
Park for several days, and the prevailing sentiment was that it
would make those not familiar with Oak Park think it was "an
awful place to live."

As another example, a police community relations officer told
an Oak Park group about one of his objections to the "Operation Whistlestop" campaign they were contemplating: "Do you
want people to say, 'Boy, is Oak Park that bad? Is it so dangerous people have to carry whistles around with them?'"

From the point of view of the community leaders and activists, all publicity had to be managed carefully, and this certainly included any publicity about an issue as volatile as crime.

Fear of crime was a convenient and powerful lever for resident involvement in community organizational life, but manipulating it required a delicate hand.

The perpetual tension between individual perceptions and the image community representatives attempted to project was evident. It was up to community leaders to maintain the positive image of community and the sense of community integrity. In the face of residents' fears of blacks, whether neighbors or outsiders, local leaders tried to define the situation as one in which the whole community stood together to ward off external threats. They attempted to manage residents' perceptions and the sources of those perceptions. In these respects Austin and Oak Park differed little. But there were important differences in the ways the communities were ultimately restructured and reconstituted, and these will be discussed below.

Reconstructing Communities

As racial change occurs, is perceived, and is defined in particular ways, the community acquires a new identity, or new means are employed to maintain the old identity. Suttles writes that residential identities are "embedded in a contrastive structure in which each neighborhood is known primarily as a counterpart to some of the others, and relative differences are probably more important than any single and widely shared social characteristic."[7]

Racial change made such symbolic distinctions even more important for community leaders in Austin and Oak Park. In Austin the result was a fission of the community into North Austin and South Austin. These could only have emerged in contrast to one another. The key distinction that gave them their separate identities was their racial composition. They became separate and distinct communities, not halves of one. In time, the term "Austin" without the designation "North" or "South" practically disappeared from use by white residents.

The original dividing line was Lake Street and the division arose when the area south of Lake Street was still predominantly white, offering an interesting example of the effect of natural boundaries on the definition of the community. It is doubtful that such a total redefinition of the community could have been sustained so far in advance of substantial racial transition without the solid barrier of the Lake Street elevated tracks, which made it easy to visualize the border.

The division of the single community into two was relatively rapid, but not abrupt. It began with increasing use of the terms North Austin and South Austin, especially by the community press. Eventually, many institutions that had been located on Lake Street moved north. Among these were the *Austinite*, the offices of one of the main community organizations, and the local alderman's office. Political redistricting reinforced the split.

When the Lake Street barrier was penetrated and substantial numbers of blacks moved into the neighborhoods to the north, Chicago Avenue became the southern limit of North Austin. This redefinition was hardly as significant as the first, however, since the community had already been split. It merely signified the continued retreat of North Austin.

The economic metaphor implied in the notion of the community of limited liability is useful in interpreting the division of Austin. The idea of limited liability draws attention to the partial and functionally specific nature of attachment to local urban communities. Such attachment is not, as earlier sociological theory suggested, based on primary ties. Rather, it represents a varying but limited investment that is contingent upon the satisfaction of certain needs and subject to withdrawal when the community ceases to meet those needs. This is the meaning of white out-migration from changing communities. Residents have varying investments in the local community, but the community leaders have special stakes not shared by ordinary residents.

The division of Austin meant that the Austin establishment had decided early to "cut its losses" by withdrawing from a large sector of the community. The leaders were not really withdrawing their investments from the community. On the contrary, they were redefining the community in an attempt to hang on to as much of their investment as possible. South Austin was "sacrificed" so that efforts might be concentrated on the "preservation" of North Austin.

While Austin residents, at least those of North Austin, accepted the new definition readily, there was more difficulty in representing Austin to the outside world as two communities. Oak Parkers, for instance, and residents of other nearby communities were aware of the distinction but took little care to observe it themselves. Austin was still perceived as a single entity. Residents of more remote communities were often unaware of the distinction. Furthermore, in perceiving Austin as one community, these outsiders also perceived it as black or changing—precisely what North Austinites had wished to avoid by constituting themselves a separate community.

The reconstruction of Oak Park did not take the form of fission of the community, although the southeast neighborhood, contiguous with South Austin, assumed a new, distinguishing identity. The phrase "southeast Oak Park" (significantly, "southeast" was not capitalized) first denoted the vaguely defined area Oak Park leaders commonly described as "sensitive" and carried omnipresent connotations of fear of racial change and potential community decline. Roughly, the boundaries of the area were the Eisenhower Expressway, Austin Boulevard, Lake Street, and Lombard Street, but the term was sometimes used to describe a larger area extending north to Chicago Avenue and west to Ridgeland. Eventually the identity of this part of the suburb was crystallized as the "East Village," although by 1977 even that designation was not used by everyone as the proper name for the neighborhood. More often it was used by community leaders to lend the area a positive aura, and it was still interchangeable with "the east side" or "east Oak Park."

Transformation of a community's identity as racial change occurs, even when the change is as moderate as in Oak Park, is probably inescapable. Racial composition is certainly one of a community's major defining symbols. Community leaders, however, have varying degrees of power to manage such symbolic identifiers and to recombine them in ways that variously affect the total image they confer. Where Austin leaders cut their losses, Oak Park leaders doubled their bets. The strategy pursued by the Oak Park leadership was not to withdraw investment in southeast Oak Park, but to commit even more resources there. The most dramatic manifestation of this commitment was the relocation of the village hall in a new civic center in southeast Oak Park. Governmental services to the East Village were increased, and augmented police patrols—including men walking beats and others patrolling on small motorcycles—led to decreases in street crime in that area after 1974.

The local government clearly took the lead in shaping the strategy for bolstering the image of Oak Park's eastern fringe. Somewhat independently, as we have already seen, the school board moved along the same strategic lines. Other institutions, perhaps most importantly the local real estate industry, followed with more trepidation. By 1975, at least a few real estate firms were practicing "affirmative marketing" of east Oak Park to whites, and a few lenders tacitly recognized racial stabilization of the area as a legitimate consideration in loan decisions, not by restricting loans to any racial group, but by leaning in the other direction to ensure that mortgage money remained available for the east side.

The presence of a local, autonomous municipal administration guarded against the splitting off of east Oak Park, since local officials were legally bound and morally committed to serve the suburb as a whole. Furthermore, the legal definition of territorial boundaries probably reinforced the informal perception of them. Territorial integrity was further enhanced by Oak Park's strong historical and cultural tradition and by the many local organizations with constituencies within the suburb's legal boundaries.

In Oak Park the establishment could not retreat and retrench as the Austin establishment did. Leaders would have found such a move nearly impossible to justify and just as difficult to effect. If they withdrew, it had to be from the whole community; and for many of them the stakes were high and their investments irreplaceable elsewhere. Positions of prestige, power, or authority within the local community hierarchy could not just be laterally transferred to other communities.

Therefore Oak Park was an indivisible whole, whereas Austin, as experience proved, was divisible. This difference had implications for the strategies the two communities adopted for handling the threat of change. Austin attempted to cope by literally excising the threat—cutting off part of the community. Oak Park, on the other hand, sought to diffuse the threat and minimize its potency by dispersing blacks throughout the community, while enhancing the reputation of that part of the community that had already drawn a concentration of black residents.

That Oak Park's identity remained whole did not mean it was any less embedded in a contrastive structure or that these contrasts were any less important in defining Oak Park. Nor did it mean that Oak Park escaped profound reconstitution as a community.

The contrastive structure in which Oak Park's identity was embedded included the newer suburbs farther west (a perceptually amorphous group that Oak Parkers alleged to have poorer services and higher taxes), as well as nearby suburbs such as Cicero, Forest Park, Elmwood Park, and Berwyn (perceived to be of lower status and rife with corruption, bigotry, or both). But the most significant counterpart in this contrastive structure was clearly Austin.

As I noted earlier, Austin and Oak Park had always competed. When Austin underwent transition, however, the contrast became even sharper and more meaningful than before. The invidious comparisons Oak Parkers had been accustomed to make began to be replaced by comments to the effect that Austin and Oak Park had really been very similar in the past. There were frequent allusions, for example, to "what a lovely neighborhood Austin used to be." An Oak Park official who had gone to school in Austin said: "We used to talk about how Oak Park was snobbish . . . but I don't know why the people of Austin should think that. It's unfortunate. Fifteen years ago, Austin and Oak Park were practically indistinguishable in physical characteristics."

It is probably true, and possibly typical of such identity-maintaining distinctions, that Austin and Oak Park were never as unlike as Oak Parkers had previously claimed or as similar as they later remembered. Minimizing past differences served to sharpen the newer and more crucial racial difference and at the same time justified the apprehensions and fears Oak Park residents felt. If Oak Park had been very like Austin, what happened in Austin could happen in Oak Park.

Given the small size of Oak Park's black population and its relative dispersal, it was far more important for Oak Park to maintain its distinction from Austin than to excise any part of its own territory. Reinforcement of this distinction was very concretely (literally and figuratively) displayed in Oak Park's plan for constructing cul-de-sacs at certain intersections. The Oak Park comprehensive plan called for all streets entering the village, except for "primary and secondary preferential streets" (usually one-half mile apart), to be blocked in that manner. While officials denied that the cul-de-sacs were racially motivated, the first to be built—and the only ones built by the summer of 1974—were on those streets intersecting Austin Boulevard between Augusta Boulevard (1000 north) and the Eisenhower Expressway. Thus the border between Oak Park and South Austin was visually and symbolically reinforced. Nonresidents of Oak Park commonly took the cul-de-sacs to be intended as racial barriers and even racial insults, and some Oak Park residents felt the same way. Some of them facetiously commented that a moat might be more effective, and the author of a letter to the *Oak Leaves* sardonically suggested that passports be required at the borders of the village. In Austin a community organization leader responded to a question on the possibility of the two communities' working together on common problems by alluding to the cul-de-sacs as evidence of Oak Park's attitude toward cooperation with Austin.

The village government also considered placing rustic-looking signposts announcing entrance into Oak Park around the borders of the suburb. A sign was first tried out at the corner of Washington and Austin boulevards. Washington Boulevard was one of the suburb's major traffic arteries, but it was also the most likely projected path of racial transition. Later the original signpost design was abandoned, and a firm was hired to devise a unified village graphics program. By 1974 a modern abstract logo had been adopted and was being displayed on large orange-and-white signs that bade one "Welcome to Oak Park." Police and other emergency vehicles were also sporting the new colors. The expense of the program was justified by the very strongly felt need to create a distinct identity for the village, one in keeping with the spirit of "the new Oak Park." Three "gateway" projects—cosmetic improvements consisting mainly of landscaping parkways and medians—at the Austin Boulevard intersections with Madison Street, Lake Street, and Chicago Avenue, further marked the boundaries.

Such visible reinforcements of community boundaries and community identity, as distinct from adjacent or nearby areas, are the identifying marks of the "defended neighborhood." They are not really so unlike the gang mottoes that grace the facades of inner-city buildings. The superficial differences between the two in style, aesthetic quality, and general social acceptability mask a common function—the designation of "turf," or the claim to legitimate proprietorship of an area. The more basic differences lie in the question of what groups or interests have the power to set, maintain, and enforce the territorial boundaries in a manner consistent with their own values, norms, and resources.

In lieu of a territorial reconstitution, Oak Park underwent a normative reconstruction. Staid, traditional Oak Park became "the new Oak Park." The new Oak Park was young, progressive, and, most important, racially integrated. It was sometimes proclaimed as an "international" or a "diverse multiethnic" community. With such characterizations, its leaders tried to create a positive evaluation of the changes taking place, and they also shifted the emphasis away from black and white to the idea of a harmonious mingling of all races and ethnic backgrounds. Although this definition was not accepted by all Oak Park residents, its mere existence was enough to distinguish that community from Austin, where integration was more frequently seen as the lesser of two evils.

Perceptual Aspects
of Black Housing
Demand

This research has not focused on perceptions and attitudes of black people in Austin, Oak Park, and the surrounding area, but these are clearly relevant to the nature of change in the two communities. Some issues can only be suggested here. For example, is the notion of "suburb" a perceptual deterrent to black people? Although the "suburban myth" has been properly debunked, the term still carries a definite connotation unlike that connoted by "city." In everyday language, the adjective "suburban" evokes images of a life-style presumably not found in the city. Part of this imagery is exclusiveness, or at least whiteness.

Thus we might properly ask whether the slow rate of black migration into Oak Park was in part a function of a habitual way of thought by blacks that defined suburbia as off limits. Fair housing leaders in Chicago have claimed that one of the major obstacles to black suburbanization has been blacks' lack of awareness that they do have wide and feasible suburban housing options. On the other hand, an ideology current among many young blacks equates moving to the suburbs with "selling out."

None of the black people with whom I spoke in the course of this research raised either of these issues in regard to the prospect of living in Oak Park or Austin. Some did believe that Oak Park was functionally closed to blacks, but the suburban issue was not raised. Others, however, thought Oak Park was more open than North Austin. There was a great deal of misinformation about housing options in both communities. For instance, one black woman, employed by a real estate agency in Austin, said she had heard blacks could neither rent nor buy homes in Oak Park, but she thought there would be no difficulty in that respect north of Chicago Avenue in Austin. This was during 1973, and just the reverse was true.

Some blacks considered Oak Park a residential option but still viewed it negatively because of their opinion that it would be-

come all black and suffer the same slum problems as South
Austin. One family moved out of the eastern edge of Oak Park
because, in the woman's words, "the trash are coming."
Another Austin black woman said she had friends in Oak Park
who had encouraged her to move there, but she was going to
wait and see whether it was going to become predominantly
black. That was in 1973. In 1974 she had made plans to move to
Rogers Park, a white community on the north side of Chicago.
An Oak Park black resident speculated:

> There are two kinds of blacks moving to the suburbs. There
> are those who are interested in schools, services, and other
> amenities, but want to retain their ties to their old commun-
> ity. Then there are the ones who break off completely.
> They're not interested in coming here. They've had old
> homes. They move way far west. As long as they're going to
> move, they want a new ranch home and a big lawn and the
> whole bit. They don't care about services, because they
> didn't have them before.

There were indications that, for many of Oak Park's blacks,
much of the suburb's desirability hinged on its remaining integrated. When two Oak Park locations were declared exempt
from the local fair housing ordinance because of substantial
black residence there, more than half of those petitioning for
exemption were black. In 1973 the village government considered enacting a law that would limit black residency to 30
percent in some sections of the village. Blacks took both sides of
this issue, as did whites. While some Oak Park blacks harshly
criticized the policy of dispersal pursued by the village, asking
why only blacks had to be dispersed, one black person probably
summed up the feelings of many in saying "When I think of the
alternative to dispersal, I'm for dispersal." A local volunteer
who had done a door-to-door survey in southeast Oak Park said
of the blacks she approached, "Let's be frank about it: they're
running, and they don't want to have to run again." Another
local fair housing leader said of the blacks who had "pioneered"
in Oak Park in the early days of open housing, "They ask if
there are any areas where blacks are concentrating or there is a

ghetto forming, and they say they want to get as far away from there as they can."

Some Oak Park leaders have stated that they believe the potential black demand in Oak Park is even greater than that in the remaining white parts of Austin, since Oak Park has gained a reputation of "openness." In 1974 the director of the Oak Park Housing Center, a housing referral service, said of the situation: "White demand has been very high, but the demand by blacks in Austin has been tremendous. It gets greater every day. It seems that every middle-class black left in Austin wants to get out."

It is likely that such economic sorting of blacks between Austin and Oak Park will continue to take place, much as it did with the earlier white migrants to the west side who populated these two communities, and that class will continue to be an important dimension of the contrast between them. This must happen if the Oak Park strategy for reshaping the village's identity is to succeed, for local leaders know that maintenance of the demand for housing by middle-class blacks as well as whites is something they cannot afford to neglect.

8

The Intervention Strategy: Austin

The process of community change as it has been described thus far was composed of a multitude of events and reactions and myriad individual and collective efforts to control and adapt to a changing residential environment. Any of these efforts might be seen as interventions in the process of change as it was perceived at given times and in given circumstances. However, in both Austin and Oak Park, there were also purposeful organized efforts aimed at modifying the course and outcome of racial change.

In Austin, two major community organizations, the Organization for a Better Austin (OBA) and the Town Hall Assembly (THA), were formed in the late 1960s to deal with the problem of racial transition.

The Organization for a Better Austin

The Organization for a Better Austin was founded in 1967 when a group of Austin clergymen concluded that the community needed a strong, active, and representative organization if it were to withstand the threat of the approaching ghetto. Almost two thousand delegates, representing a variety of local groups and institutions, attended the community congress called in 1967. That congress ratified the proposal to form a permanent organization, and OBA was the result.

OBA was an umbrella group that eventually claimed a membership of more than 180 black, white, and interracial associations ranging from churches to block clubs. This figure should be interpreted with caution, however, for OBA sometimes counted as members groups that merely sent representatives to its annual open meeting, even including groups thoroughly at odds with OBA.

Each year at that meeting, a new board of officers was elected and a new program formulated. In 1973 OBA had three full-time, salaried staff members and several community organizers who had been assigned to OBA as trainees by various other organizations and institutions. The formal leadership of OBA consisted of five senior officers and seventeen vice-presidents, each of whom headed a committee. From the beginning, clergy and religious were notably present among the officers, trainees, and volunteer staff.

OBA's wide-ranging program and ad hoc approach involved it in issues that at one time or another had implications for most of Austin's residents. This facet of the organization gave it a more or less floating membership, as people participated in the issues of most direct concern to them.

At the first all-Austin congress in 1967, the following resolutions, designed to stabilize community life in Austin, were adopted: (1) support for low-density zoning, (2) support for better police control of Cicero Avenue, and (3) inauguration of a campaign to attract white families to Austin. The last one represented OBA's major thrust for the first three years of its operation. OBA waged a campaign against panic-peddling and operated a housing referral service. The strategy was to discourage whites from moving out of the changing or fringe areas and to encourage blacks to look for housing in all-white areas that lay well beyond the immediate site of racial transition. OBA claimed to have placed more than two thousand white applicants in homes and apartments south of Lake Street, but it had little success in placing blacks in outlying white neighborhoods and suburbs or in discouraging them from moving into the changing and fringe neighborhoods. OBA could not, by itself, open up the white neighborhoods to black occupancy. Furthermore, it was competing with the many private real estate firms that were more than willing to place black families in the fringe areas.

Undoubtedly, other factors also contributed to the eventual demise of the OBA housing referral service. When questioned about why it had ceased operation, a spokesman said that, though it had been the "most successful such service in the city," it had been difficult to operate because of "manpower shortages." A former OBA president said that severe crowding in the schools of southern Austin had driven white families out and precluded finding other white families to replace them.

During OBA's first year of operation, a major accomplishment was the Chicago school board's agreement to bus school-children from two overcrowded and largely black southeast Austin schools to white schools with ample space. In 1968, when the program began, 317 children from May School and 256 from Spencer School were bused to eight schools in hostile white working-class neighborhoods on the northwest side of the city, including northern Austin.

Passing years saw a shift in OBA priorities. Before 1970, more emphasis was given to racial stabilization and to the effort to attract white families to Austin. Later, posttransitional problems such as crime, deteriorating housing, and the flight of financial institutions received greater attention.

In 1973 OBA was still concerned about overcrowding in the area schools. Busing, demountables, mobile units, and physical plant additions were all used to deal with the problem. OBA took credit for having brought in the many demountables. OBA was also largely responsible for convincing the Board of Education to purchase an abandoned Catholic school building to be used as a branch for Austin High School, relieving the main plant of one thousand students, and OBA pressure was instrumental in the construction of two middle schools in Austin.

Despite its continuing interest in the area's school problems, however, OBA began to put more emphasis on housing. Aban-

doned buildings were a growing problem in Austin. The following newspaper account describes the action OBA took on
one occasion:

> By order of a kangaroo building court held on the bed of a
> rented truck, Austin area residents yesterday launched an
> assault on an abandoned building in their neighborhood.
> The self-appointed judge... (dressed in a dark robe re-
> sembling a judge) signaled the beginning of the effort with
> a raised fist, the drop of a sledge hammer, and a loud cheer.
> Accompanied by shouts of "right on" the "jury"...
> marched toward a vacant house at 1652 W. Ohio St.,
> which OBA officials said they had unsuccessfully asked
> the city building department to tear down.[1]

There was a diminishing focus on panic-peddling as OBA
began to perceive that the most formidable enemy was not the
small-time operator, but the entire real estate and lending industry and its auxiliary institutions and agencies. OBA vigorously opposed FHA financing of buildings in need of major
repairs, and it tried to force FHA to reimburse buyers for repairs made on FHA-approved housing with extensive code
violations. OBA also fought the policy of redlining. The organization worked to prevent financial institutions from leaving the
area, and in July 1973 one Austin savings and loan firm was
denied its request to relocate in the suburbs, largely as a result
of OBA pressure.

A marked shift in OBA policy was the reorientation of the
group's aims to meet the needs of the black community. OBA's
leadership also began to reflect that shift. After 1972, OBA
presidents were black, and there was much more black participation at all levels. As the neighborhoods underwent transition, OBA made a similar one.

One facet that did not change was OBA's style. Its first director had trained under Saul Alinsky, and the group took on and
retained an Alinskyite character. Following Alinsky's principles, OBA's strategies were based on confrontation and conflict,
inciting residents to action through emotional and self-
interested appeals and tailoring the means to the specific ends.
Critics sometimes said the tactics were designed to rub the

wounds of society raw; or, as a Chicago Commission on Human Relations official was quoted, "OBA tactics are to keep their feet up the government's ass."[2]

Most of the time, OBA tried to meet directly with those against whom they had complaints—usually landlords, real estate men, or city officials—to arrive at some agreement. However, OBA members were also reputed to take matters into their own hands if resolutions did not meet expectations. Several incidents blemished OBA's already shaky image in the community. In 1970, for instance, an OBA vice-president was charged with arson (though later acquitted), in a fire that damaged the office of Sky Realty, one of OBA's major foes. In an article by Franklin Dunlap appearing in the *Chicago Tribune Magazine*, an OBA supporter was reported to have said:

> The fire-bombing of the Sky office—You bet we did it. A woman did it, as a matter of fact, threw it right thru the window and burned the bastards out. Not the woman the cops got and charged with arson, then found not guilty. Cops were all wet on that broad, but I ain't telling precisely *who* she was. She was careful, she checked it out good, and there was no one living upstairs or anything. We just burned out those creeps' real estate office. Real estate people here in Austin'll do anything to make a goddamned dime, but we got them that time and burned them out. They deserve everything they get.[3]

The following year, the Chicago Commission on Human Relations found an OBA vice-president guilty of panic-peddling. He had sent area homeowners a letter that stated:

> You probably bought a home in Austin for the same reason many of us did—excellent transportation and a stable residential community away from the loop but not miles out in the suburbs.
>
> Some things are starting to change, however. Many people are complaining about crowded schools, declining city services, etc. Some of these problems can be traced to the rapid turnover from white to black in Austin.

The complaint had been filed by a vice-president of the Town Hall Assembly, who contended that OBA was subject to

panic-peddling charges because it acted as a real estate agent
through its housing referral service, though the intent of the
letter quoted above was to get people involved in community
action and hardly to drive white residents away. In Dunlap's
article, a real estate broker also commented on OBA's participation in the real estate business in Austin:

> Listen, I sold pots and pans once, and I called regularly on
> this whorehouse. Well, I got to know the girls, and there was
> Eunice who lived above the whorehouse. She was married,
> but when her husband was off at work, she would drop
> down occasionally and turn a trick for spending money. I
> came in one day, and Eunice and this other whore were
> having at each other, one with a bottle and one with a knife.
> One of the girls grabbed one, and the pimp got between them,
> and I tried to make light of it. "What's this world comin' to,"
> I said, "if we can't even trust two whores to be nice to each
> other?" Eunice got real indignant. "Don't call me no whore!"
> she said. "She's the whore. I do it just for spending money,
> and she's full-time!" You see?...O.B.A. is like Eunice.[4]

The panic-peddling case was not the first time OBA had tried
to arouse citizens' interest by manipulating the fear of racial
change. Following the premise that the way to mobilize people
is to appeal to their self-interest and their emotions, OBA did
not hesitate to play on the presumed racism of white Austinites.
One of its meeting announcements, for example, read, "On
[date] a black family moved into [address]. Will this happen on
your block?" At the same time, however, OBA was working
closely with black block clubs in southern Austin. OBA missed
the target on two counts. First, by attempting to work with both
a black and a white constituency, it raised confusion about its
motives. It was suspected by some of deceit and duplicity. Although OBA had tried to define the situation so that the interests of the two groups were compatible, many whites, and
possibly many blacks as well, failed to be convinced. Second, the
blatant racism of some of the appeals was offensive to white
Austinites, who knew when they were being talked down to.
They were not liberals by any means, but neither did they consider themselves bigots.

OBA was also accused by some area businessmen of using intimidation to extort contributions. OBA denied being involved in any violence, but picketing and demonstrating were among its major tactics. A businessman reportedly said that an OBA delegation had asked him for $1,500 and left with shouts of "pay up or get out," and another complained that he was told to contribute $500 or his place of business would be picketed: "I really don't know what to call them; dues I guess. We paid them $250 because we're vulnerable."[5] The operator of a small restaurant was quoted as saying, "They came to see me and they had a price on my head."[6]

Even when OBA's tactics were clearly within the law, they were suspect to many of Austin's generally conservative white residents. OBA picketed the homes and churches of real estate men whom they accused of panic-peddling. They harassed landlords into making repairs and real estate agents into giving refunds. An OBA handbill describes one of their methods:

> John Liutgaarden, of Sky Real Estate, promised us he would fix up Mrs. Edwards' house completely. All he has done is unstop the sewer. Mrs. Edwards is left with thousands of dollars in repair work. We want Sky Real Estate to finish the repairs—bad wiring—rotten window frames— rotten bathroom floor.
>
> Call John Liutgaarden at 275-3400 and tell him to fix Mrs. Edwards' house.

Such tactics were often effective, but they also cost OBA much support in the community. Apparently OBA considered the trade-off worthwhile.

The Town Hall Assembly

Austin's second major community organization, and OBA's archrival, was the Town Hall Assembly. Composed of approximately sixty-five member organizations in the area surrounding the Town Hall and bounded by Long, Austin, Lake, and Chicago, the THA was founded soon after OBA in 1967 and is perhaps best understood as a reaction to OBA.

Strictly a volunteer agency and manned entirely by Austin residents, THA did not consider OBA the grass-roots organization it claimed to be, because of the "outsiders" and professional organizers or organizer trainees connected with it.

A THA officer said THA was formed to provide a "catalyst" for the block clubs arising in the central part of Austin, not as an opposition group to OBA. But the obvious implication was that OBA was not fulfilling the need. In addition to block clubs and other organizations within THA's boundaries, Austin groups with recognized interests in the Town Hall area were also eligible to join. Unlike OBA, THA was supported by and worked in close alliance with Austin's major community institutions, such as the Austin Business Council, various fraternal and service organizations, and the *Austinite* weekly newspaper. In fact, from the outset THA enjoyed a near monopoly on the center of Austin, geographically, institutionally, and ideologically. It was of the establishment and worked through the establishment, leading to accusations by opponents that it was a tool manipulated by local politicians and businessmen.

THA's original major goal, like that of OBA, was to stablize the community racially. Yet THA did not set up a housing referral service, for, as a spokeswoman said, "There is already one in every Catholic church in the area." This statement beautifully illustrates the extent to which THA was bound up with the traditional, largely informal, church-centered social network, for none of the churches had formally organized housing services, though some had bulletin boards or phone numbers to call for housing information. A similarly revealing comment was made by a THA officer when she was asked to explain OBA's success in organizing black residents of South Austin. "They're just moving in," she said, "and they're confused. They don't know their way around yet." That is, they did not know how things got done in Austin, for they had not had time to become acquainted with the proper channels and procedures.

THA also did not devise programs for monitoring code violations in buildings or keeping an eye on real estate practices. A THA sympathizer characterized such programs as "snooping around." THA was inclined to minimize such problems, and it scorned OBA's claims of their prevalence. Said an officer of THA about the OBA programs, "They create problems so organizer trainees can get their experience."[7] Rather than real estate practices, THA emphasized schools as the key to stabilizing Austin. One of the group's major aims was to restore Austin High School boundaries to their pre-1964 location. In the absence of a boundary change, THA worked to open alternatives for Austin's white high school students. For example, THA pressure was largely responsible for getting out-of-district Lane Technical High School opened to Austin district students, and it also campaigned successfully for a permissive transfer program to allow students to attend other out-of-district high schools. It had demanded, but had not received, a new high school for North Austin. To accomplish such ends, THA worked arduously but quietly with the Board of Education and other city agencies, never utilizing what one THA volunteer called "yelling, kangaroo-court tactics"—an obvious reference to OBA.

THA's program included working with local employers to encourage their employees to seek housing in Austin. It also supported the proposed "crosstown expressway," which would probably run along Austin's eastern border, entailing the demolition of some of Austin's most deteriorated structures and the displacement of some of Austin's black population. The latter was the precise reason OBA had opposed the expressway project, and this policy difference indicates some of the difference in the constituencies and ultimate values to which the two groups addressed themselves.

THA was responsible for the lowering of Austin's property tax assessment. For a number of years it ran a tutoring program in reading and math for local schoolchildren. It sponsored a drug program and generally tried to encourage better communication between the police and the area's youth. It also conducted a public relations program designed to promote a positive image of Austin and to counteract what it felt was the negative image of the community projected by OBA's complaints. A THA vice-president was quoted as saying:

OBA claims they want stability in Austin, but they only get bad publicity for it. I get flyers from OBA. If I didn't know better, I'd say, My God, this must be a terrible place. I'd move out. It is demoralizing to have picketing in your community, and these flyers they are always sending out—this is not conducive to residential living. There is a lot to be proud of in Austin, beautiful homes and beautiful architecture.... We have rich and we have poor, but THA wants to attract middle-class people to this area. Our methodology is very different from OBA's. We have positive programs while OBA takes a germ of truth and exploits it.[8]

THA tried to get as much press and television coverage as it could, but it never succeeded in matching what OBA received. Within the community it helped sponsor holiday parades and such events as the "Old Austin Days" festival. Even an OBA representative conceded ironically: "THA does things this community needs. They have a parade, they have dinner dances, the nice and healthy things. Things OBA doesn't have time to do."[9]

THA was a thoroughly establishment-oriented group, with close ties to the local business community, politicians, and the community press and a commitment to going through channels. In THA's view, real estate and lending officials were mostly honest, respectable businessmen who performed vital functions for the community. Members of these professions made financial contributions to THA and served on its board, and a local bank sometimes provided meeting space.

THA never took a policy stance that was openly segregationist. In fact, officers pointed with some pride to the few blacks involved in the organization. Some leaders hoped, at least privately, that North Austin might remain white, but few if any counted on it. For THA, clinging to the time-honored ways of getting things done, the tide of change was coming overwhelmingly fast.

Interorganizational Relations

The relations between OBA and THA were rancorous. It was not by chance that the panic-peddling charge against the OBA officer was filed by a THA officer. On one occasion THA called the police to eject some OBA people from a THA meeting. An OBA member's view of the conflict was this:

> THA says we only cause dissension in Austin, but if it weren't for our activism, THA wouldn't exist. They exist only to attack everything we do. They favored busing until OBA backed it, and then they opposed. But THA is not even public. They have their token blacks while we work with blacks and they work with us. THA has a buzzer on their door. You have to buzz to get in like a funky private club, and that screams fear to me.[10]

An OBA member told me:

> I think we have the same aims, but everything we do, they're against. Sometimes I think they just exist to be against us. They're working with the realtors. . . . To me a realtor is the enemy. He has to prove otherwise. He's not a friend till he proves himself an enemy—he's an enemy until he proves himself a friend. They're all alike.

It was not just the real estate men, the landlords, and the THA who seemed to be OBA's enemies. OBA appeared to avoid any cooperative ties with established organizations and interests. The Leadership Council for Metropolitan Open Communities (a metropolitan fair housing group), the Chicago Commission on Human Relations, and the Department of Registration and Education (which licenses real estate brokers) were just a few of the organizations that at one time or another found themselves on the receiving end of OBA's wrath. Representatives of such groups might find their offices jammed with OBA supporters demanding a meeting, or they might be invited to meetings in the Austin community where they would be bitterly castigated and usually shouted down when they defended themselves. Needless to say, OBA made few influential friends. It held to its conviction that pressure from "the people" could make the system responsive.

The conflict extended from the leadership level down to the most peripheral supporters of OBA and THA. For example, one woman complained, nearly in tears, that she had attended an OBA meeting and consequently had been ostracized by her neighbors. She lived in THA's central Austin stronghold, which OBA was never able to crack. OBA's attempts to organize there only succeeded in generating more hostility against them.

Austin's two umbrella organizations, therefore, were entirely different in character and in strategy, and those differences led to the marked hostility between them. OBA supporters generally considered THA ineffective and cemented to the status quo, while THA partisans considered OBA leaders to be "outside agitators," devious and divisive in their tactics.

It seemed that OBA had misread the character of the Austin community. Its aggressive flamboyance and its attempts to play on racial fears to get white Austinites involved failed to contend with the fact that overt race prejudice was contrary to the prevailing self-image of Austin's residents. They resented being characterized as bigots.

Many Austinites viewed OBA's involvement with both pro- and anti-integrationist constituencies as hypocrisy or as self-serving agitation by people who had no deep or lasting interest in the community, though this was hardly fair to the many Austin residents who devoted great amounts of time to the organization. However, the indigenous social network and leadership in Austin had been largely bypassed in the formation of OBA. OBA's bringing in outside organizers was a source of deep community resentment. Many Austinites also rejected OBA's militancy and considered the group "radical," though philosophically, if not tactically, it was anything but.[11]

OBA's underlying premise was that Austin was a community in the process of racial change and that the change would result in a new social character and new needs. But this premise was not generally accepted by white residents of North Austin. The North Austin establishment, which included THA, operated on the theory that Austin had become two social and territorial communities. Rather than change its conception of the general social and cultural character of the community and redefine its values and norms, the Austin establishment decided to redraw and, if necessary, keep on redrawing the shrinking boundaries within which its old values held sway.

OBA might have been considered an organization ahead of

its time. At the beginning, it did not fit the community in which it operated. Only after much racial transition had occurred could the *Austinite* editorialize that "Austin was forced to accept OBA tactics only because of its extreme frustration with regular channels, but it did not like or approve them." OBA's Alinskyite character could have been embraced by Austinites only at the specific time when they perceived that they were in a fight for territorial survival. Unfortunately for them, by this time much of Austin had already changed from white to black.

THA fit white Austin's self-concept to a much greater degree than did OBA. THA moved in ways white Austinites considered proper. It did not engage in shouting matches with public officials. It never aired the community's dirty linen in public, and it never embarrassed the community. It was an organization of local people who behaved in a "rational" manner. THA stressed the positive reasons for staying in or moving to Austin: the beautiful homes and other amenities found there. It maintained an aloof, dignified profile, far removed from the turbulence of reality. But the very characteristics of THA that appealed to Austinites doomed the organization to weakness. By trying to preserve the status quo, THA failed to come to grips with the rapid racial change that overtook Austin.

Therefore, both of the community organizations set up to stabilize Austin failed—one partly because it could not generate community acceptance until it was too late to test its tactics, the other partly because saving Austin's public face took priority over developing an action-oriented program. Whether either of them might have otherwise succeeded against the long odds prevailing is moot.

9

Intervention in Oak Park: Local Government

In Oak Park, the response to anticipated racial change differed greatly from that in Austin, by the variety of groups involved, by the nature of the relations among them, and by the immensely important role played by the local authorities.

Unlike Austin, Oak Park had an autonomous municipal government, which became one of the central forces in the fight to achieve racial stability. The links between government, quasi-governmental bodies such as school boards, and voluntary organizations were complex. In contrast to the segmented character of the organizational response in Austin, the response to racial change in Oak Park was mediated through a loosely coherent network of groups that I will discuss at greater length in the next chapter. Furthermore, the plethora of administrative and service bureaucracies, which in Austin were external agents to be battled or bargained with, were in Oak Park the internal loci of substantial resources to be directed with relative ease toward the goal of racial stability. Practically every local governmental agency and administrative authority had some role to play in the overall effort to stabilize the community racially.

The Oak Park village government, headed by the village president and the six-member board of trustees, controlled the greatest resources for intervention in the process of change. It had money, competence, organization, and legal authority, and it was accorded a high level of respect and legitimacy by its citizens.

The most important levers available to the village government were legislation, through which it could exert control over the real estate industry and affect directly and indirectly the occupancy, type, and cost of housing in the village; management of public works and physical development projects, which were used to project a tangible representation of the community's identity and to create through physical design what Oscar Newman has termed "defensible space";[1] and distribution of routine public goods and services, meted out in a way intended to enhance the residential environment of east Oak Park. The last two of these leverage mechanisms have been discussed already. Cul-de-sacs and "gateways" set the village apart from the city of Chicago. The seat of government was moved to southeast Oak Park to show commitment to that neighborhood, and police protection and other services there were upgraded. The "Frank Lloyd Wright Historic Preservation District" was already in existence, and plans for a second historic district containing some of the suburb's oldest homes and representing the Victorian Queen Anne and Italianate architectural styles was being planned. Downtown, the shopping mall had been built, funded by a special taxing district permitted under the village's home rule powers, newly granted under the 1971 Illinois Constitution. A comprehensive plan for the village had also been completed, aimed at revitalizing Oak Park both physically and economically.

Such measures were considered essential to renewing and maintaining middle-class demand for housing in Oak Park, an obviously important ingredient of racial stability. However, the village government also took steps to intervene directly in the process of racial change, through various types of real-estate control legislation and through official organs created to manage integration. These more direct tools and the way they were used are the primary concern of this chapter.

While the most important of the particular tactics employed are described individually here, it is important not to lose sight of the pattern by which the local governmental response evolved. In the eight years beginning with the 1968 municipal fair housing ordinance, the official intervention strategy changed from one characterized by caution, informal persuasion, and minimal direct control to one that was greatly expanded in its scope, was given central priority among governmental functions, and relied much more heavily than before on formal sanctions as opposed to pressure and persuasion and on expertise as opposed to informal local ties. Although only the board of trustees had the power to pass legislation, much of the business of government, including the deliberation over, drafting of, and ultimate enforcement of legislation, took place at the level of the appointed citizens' advisory commissions. The Community Relations Commission was most directly involved in the control of the real estate industry and the housing market, and it also functioned as a central coordinator for the variety of auxiliary tactics aimed at manipulating a stably integrated community.

The Community Relations Commission was a fifteen-member body created in 1963. Although its formation had been discussed for some time before that, the immediate precipitant was the firing of a newly hired black musician by the Oak Park Symphony Orchestra, for reasons rumored to be racial. During the next few years, a small but strong pro–civil rights contingent was developing in Oak Park and making its influence and representation felt. But, in the absence of such immediate and inescapably local spurs to action as had prompted the Community Relations Commission's formation, five years passed before local authorities again confronted the issue of race in a direct and immediate way.

In May 1968, after weeks of heated debate and stormy public hearings, the village board passed a fair housing ordinance. The ordinance prohibited discrimination in home and apartment advertising, sales, rentals, and financing. It outlawed panic-peddling and prohibited real estate agents from approaching homeowners who had notified the village government that they did not wish to be solicited for the sale of their homes.

The law required anyone engaged in real estate business in Oak Park to obtain a license from the village clerk (a provision later found by the state supreme court to be unconstitutional in a suit involving other suburbs). The ordinance was generally considered a strong one, not so much because of the $500 fine levied for violation as because it provided injunctive powers—an essential enforcement tool that many municipal fair housing laws lacked. The law also contained a provision, referred to as the "exempt location clause," whereby the village government could exempt particular sites from prosecution, in the interest of preserving racial balance. This was to be a safeguard against resegregation.

Although the Community Relations Commission was charged with administering the ordinance, it did not gain an office or staff until 1970, when a half-time administrator and full-time secretary were appointed. The major responsibility of the community relations staff was to act on complaints of fair housing law violations. Legitimate complaints that could not be conciliated were passed on for commission action and then forwarded to the village attorney for prosecution. The aim, however, was conciliation. From June 1970 through December 1971, the community relations staff received thirty-four complaints, of which eighteen were dismissed by the administrator for lack of substance or complainant disinterest, eleven were satisfactorily conciliated, and five were prosecuted. Except for one, all the complaints were of alleged discrimination in apartment rentals. The exception was a charge against a broker who was operating his office without a license and in a residentially zoned area. The pattern set during this first eighteen-month period changed little. There were no complaints of discrimination in home sales until the summer of 1973, when the managers of a condominium building were accused of refusing to sell a unit to a couple from India, and a River Forest broker was charged with racial steering.

There were other charges of racial steering after 1973, resulting in suspension of the licenses of five Berwyn and Cicero brokerage firms. In 1975 Oak Park joined with three other suburbs and the Leadership Council for Metropolitan Open Communities as plaintiffs in a suit in federal court charging a total of fourteen firms with racial discrimination and illegal steering. The five mentioned above, whose licenses had already been suspended by the Illinois Department of Registration and Education, were among the defendants. None of the six firms alleged in the suit to have steered white clients out of Oak Park were based in Oak Park. Therefore this ultimately successful suit was an important test of the local government's capacity to control the practices of firms beyond its own municipal jurisdiction. If the village could deal firmly and expeditiously with real estate dealers from outside the community, it would be well on the way to having the real estate situation under control; for the Oak Park brokers were largely compliant with the local government's nondiscrimination measures.

As Oak Park residents and leaders increasingly perceived and reacted to black in-migration in the southeast sector of the community, the community relations staff's communication, coordination, and record-keeping functions became more important. The staff was available for continuous monitoring and for immediate intervention in tension-producing situations. It handled inquiries and attempted to quell rumors. It was able to coordinate activities and programs relating to racial stabilization among other village departments and official bodies. At least until 1973, it kept up-to-date records on black move-ins, although after 1973 community relations officials claimed they no longer recorded them.

The commission staff also initiated some programs of its own. In the fall of 1971 it began its counseling program, intended to discourage blacks from moving into blocks where other blacks already lived and where white anxiety over racial change was judged to be high. When local brokers had black prospects for homes in such blocks, they were asked to refer them to the community relations administrator, who would then encourage them to seek housing in some other part of Oak Park.

The counseling program was a somewhat sensitive subject for commission members and staff. The staff did not seem willing to speak freely about it and sought no publicity for it. They were bothered by the discrimination implicit in the fact that only minorities were counseled. They were trying to work out a way to counsel white prospects as well without frightening them away from the southeast part of the village. A commission member complained that the counseling program had "grown up like Topsy," pursued by the staff but out of the control of the commission itself. In all fairness to the commission staff, the commissioners had shown no eagerness to involve themselves in it. It was a program that had to work inconspicuously if it were to work at all. By 1974 the direction had changed to the extent that community relations personnel were counseling mostly whites who were interested in southeast Oak Park homes but were vacillating. They estimated that about 1 percent of the village's home-buyers were then being counseled. Later, as the single-family home market appeared to stabilize, emphasis again shifted to counseling prospective black tenants of east side apartment buildings.

The low profile the commissioners initially maintained for the counseling program was indicative of their dilemma at that stage of racial change. The administrator had half-facetiously characterized his work as "how to succeed without really trying." The question was, more specifically, how to deal with a perceived problem without calling attention to the problem's existence. The commission was also well aware that on an issue as volatile as race, nearly any action or stand it took was likely to draw criticism from some quarter. Added to this was the uncertainty stemming from the lack of any model for successful intervention in the process of racial change and the difficulty of predicting the consequences of any action.

The cautious mood of the Community Relations Commission was apparent at its January 1972 meeting, when the commissioners were forced to commit themselves to a stand they would have preferred to keep off the record. The joint governing board of the prestigious First Congregational and First Presbyterian churches had received a request from a local activist for office space for a proposed "housing center," or housing referral service, aimed at promoting a dispersed pattern of racial integration throughout the village. A delegation from the churches was sent to the commission meeting to obtain its opinion on the proposal. Although one delegate pointed out that the opinion of the commission would not be binding on them, the delegates behaved with marked deference toward the commission, and it was clear that considerable weight would be attached to its judgment. One of the delegates said she felt that whatever was done in the area of human relations should be done "with the blessings of the Community Relations Commission as the official body." There was a long discussion that revealed the commission's ambivalence over how direct and aggressive a role it should assume. At first some of the commissioners seemed taken aback by the housing center proposal, as it was pointed out that the Citizens' Committee for Human Rights (the local, voluntary fair housing group) had urged the commission to operate just such a service from a storefront in the summer of 1971. Without explicitly refusing, the commission had taken no action on the suggestion. It had in effect tabled the idea because, the chairman said, "We felt at the time the important thing was diffusion out into all parts of the community, rather than concentration in a localized area, which could draw criticism." The commission's motivation clearly was still to avoid drawing criticism, although some of the commissioners were beginning to grow restless under the self-imposed restraint. The need for public trust and the need to avoid controversy made the commission reluctant to go on record as backing any volunteer efforts, even though they were not under the official auspices of the village government. One commissioner spoke of the danger of "persons getting into this work who do not know what they are doing," and later he asked his fellow commissioners, "But how would you feel about outsiders picking up the ball and running with it?"

Despite considerable soul-searching over the role of the commission and its limitations and over the advantages and perils of volunteer efforts, it was evident early in the debate that most of the commissioners were in favor of the housing center. They just did not want to give it their formal endorsement. Several times, when discussion ebbed, the chairman turned to the church delegation to ask if they had heard enough to make their report. Each time, the delegates pressed for a more explicit statement from the commission. Finally a resolution was introduced by a new commissioner who was attending her first meeting. After considerable rewording, a resolution was passed recommending that the churches act favorably on the housing center request. The chairman prefaced the calling of the vote with, "We'll go through this procedure we go through about twice a year," thus perhaps combining a final statement of his reluctance with some gentle instruction to the new member who had introduced the motion.

At a subsequent commission meeting, a commissioner who had been absent when that resolution was passed fulfilled the very fears implicit in the group's reluctance to make the endorsement. He asked, "Is it the policy for the Community Relations Commission, an arm of the village government, to endorse this kind of aggressive action to attract people to this community? This is the policy of the Board of Trustees?"

This incident was one of the clearest examples of the dilemma with which the commissioners were struggling. They were just beginning to feel rather painfully the need to address a very controversial issue without raising controversy. This period marked a turning point, after which the community relations commissioners and the village trustees became increasingly committed to more and more active and direct intervention.

In February 1972 the village board passed an ordinance banning "for sale" and "sold" signs from all residential property other than condominiums and newly constructed units. The ordinance had been proposed in the fall of 1971, but it had been returned by the Board of Trustees to the Community Relations Commission for further study, an action that was construed as rejection. When several months of deliberation with real estate board representatives failed to produce a voluntary sign-limitation program, the commission again voted to have an ordinance drafted and sent to the trustees. This time the measure was passed immediately.

The commission was operating with a growing sense of urgency, produced less by existing conditions than by anticipation of the summer moving months. While the commission still hesitated to focus attention on southeast Oak Park, for fear of stigmatizing the area, residents of that area were calling for visible indications of commitment from the village government. Pressure for action was coming from within the commission as well, and remarks like those below, made by commissioners, were variations on a recurring theme:

> The time factor is crucial.
> Time is running out.
> Time is of the essence.
> We have a summer which is going to be hot and heavy as far as housing is concerned.
> The time for us to act is now.

In 1972 three additional positions were created on the community relations staff, including a full-time administrator. With the appointment of the new administrator came a reorganization of the office. The Oak Park Community Relations Department, under control of the village manager, was created in place of the former Community Relations Commission staff. The commission continued in its role as an advisory body and retained its authority to conduct formal hearings on alleged fair housing violations.

The first community relations administrator had been a local man with strong ties to local real estate brokers. Their high regard for him had been one of his greatest assets in eliciting their cooperation, which he had done with exemplary success. The new administrator was chosen specifically for his competence and expertise in community relations work and was recruited from a nationwide field of candidates.

The new style of leadership was illustrative of the village's new direction in community and race relations. The community relations function was being expanded, elevated in status, centralized, and professionalized. It was completing its gradual move from the periphery of municipal government activity to its center, a shift paralleled by the moving of the Community Relations Department office from the municipal annex building to the main floor of the village hall. Its hours were also extended to evenings and weekends. A month before the new administrator was to begin work, one of the staff predicted that community relations policy would get tougher under the new, reorganized administration: "It's time to let the rental agents know we mean business. It's been three years. They've had plenty of time to be educated. They know what the law is. We don't have to educate them any more."

Between August and October 1972 there were a series of revisions of and amendments to the fair housing law. One of these specifically outlawed redlining. This provision, approved in spite of the objections of the local lenders, was the culmination of the concern that had been growing for more than a year. Those working for stabilization had remained convinced that redlining was going on, even though no substantial evidence had been found.

Another area of increasing concern was the practice of steering white buyers out of southeast Oak Park and black buyers into that area. Some of the community relations commissioners had urged that the commission undertake covert "testing" to determine the extent of both steering and redlining, but it had been the general feeling of the commission that such testing was not within its mandate. By the spring of 1973 the mood had changed so much that the commission voted to begin a testing program. This step was all the more dramatic in that it put the commission in direct confrontation with the newly elected Board of Trustees, which held to the position that it was not the proper function of a government body and that it would result in harassment of local businessmen. However, in a joint meeting of the trustees and commissioners, the trustees gave in to the commission on the condition that evidence derived from testing would not be used for prosecution.

Before the matter was so peacefully settled, however, the dispute over testing had been an angry one. The commission took the village board's position as an outright challenge to its autonomy. The situation was not eased by the fact that the trustees had publicly communicated their firm rejection of the policy of testing before the board had even met with the Community Relations Commission. This left the commissioners even more offended. The commission took the stand that it would go ahead with a testing program no matter what the trustees said. On the other hand, one of the trustees was alleged to have said that if the commission proceeded with a testing program, he would vote to withdraw its funding. Thus the first joint meeting between the board and the commission turned out to be anticlimactic after all the bitter exchanges preceding it, and the compromise seemed to appease all parties.

Monitoring of real estate practices, which had been such a controversial issue in 1973, became routine procedure by the following year. Between September 1974 and March 1976, more than 120 such tests were conducted, and although none of the handful of cases of apparent steering by local firms ended up in court, a CRD staff member held that prosecution was indeed a course of action available to the village if testing uncovered discriminatory policies.[2]

The controversy attending the inauguration of testing reveals the increasing level of conflict that was a by-product of other trends in the evolution of the community relations function in the village. Already that function had been split between the commission and the department. Removing the staff from the control of the advisory commission was a step away from the highly valued ideal of citizen participation. It also left the role of the commission in question, since without a staff to direct it was relegated to a strictly advisory capacity. The magnitude of its role was thus even more dependent upon the position taken by the village board; hence, the sharp reaction when its role seemed in danger of being diminished.

It was clear from the beginning that the new village board elected in April 1973 intended to involve itself more actively and directly in the stabilization effort than had past boards, which tended to refer most relevant matters to the Community Relations Commission. Its first act of business was to adopt a resolution entitled "Maintaining Diversity in Oak Park." It was the first formal statement of an official policy of "dispersal," described as follows:

Efforts to achieve diversity are nullified by the resegregation of neighborhoods from all white to all black. We, individually and as a community, have worked long and hard on behalf of open housing in Oak Park; we must not succumb to Big-City-style residential patterns.

A free and open community—equal and diverse—can only be achieved through dispersal: a mixture of racial and ethnic groups throughout the Village.

The resolution set the tone for things to come. The village board began to take the initiative in the racial stabilization effort, sometimes independent of and sometimes even at odds with the Community Relations Commission.

In November 1973 one block and one apartment building, each with over 50 percent black occupancy, were granted exemption from prosecution under the local fair housing ordinance. The exempt location clause had been included in the ordinance largely to make the law acceptable to many in the community who feared that opening the door to black residents would also open the door to racial transition. Many of the ordinance's supporters never expected the provision to be used. The village government's invocation of the clause may be seen as a continuation of the trend toward more direct intervention in the real estate market. But while most of the official action up to this point had aimed at enforcing nondiscrimination, this was the village government's first open and deliberate move in the other direction, amounting to selective discrimination rather than totally open housing. This was to become a main issue dividing those government bodies involved in managing integration in ensuing years and a source of intermittent conflict among the Board of Trustees, the Community Relations Department, and the Community Relations Commission.

The actions of the Board of Trustees beginning with the exempt location move made it clear that dispersal was to be interpreted in practice as halting resegregation on the east side. That is, priority was to be given to controlling the rate of black in-migration there. However, some members of both the Community Relations Department and the Community Relations Commission believed that greater emphasis should be placed on opening up the all-white apartment buildings on the west side of Oak Park. When it was first issued, the community relations director had assailed the board's 1973 resolution on dispersal as a disguised appeal for maintaining not diversity, as the document said, but the status quo. "Maintaining" integration, he argued, was impossible because Oak Park was not yet integrated—it was a white community. He, in turn, was sharply criticized by a trustee for allegedly failing to follow the board's directive on dispersal.

In 1975 a Community Relations Commission report called for primary program emphasis on integrating all-white buildings. The debate continued and the dilemma remained unresolved, for although few leaders felt that Oak Park could afford totally open housing, many found distasteful the overtly discriminatory measures that seemed to be required to prevent resegregation, and they knew that in employing them they were walking a legal tightrope.

The most hotly debated of such measures was a proposed racial quota that went far beyond the scope of the exempt location provision—itself of questionable legality. The granting of exempt location permitted discrimination, at least under local law, but it did not prevent sale or rental of units to blacks in any area. In December 1973 a village trustee proposed to do just that by enacting a quota ordinance limiting black occupancy in southeast Oak Park to 30 percent. This became the most controversial issue in village politics since the fair housing ordinance itself. Both blacks and whites aligned themselves on each side of the issue. A community newspaper and a local church conducted polls, and each found the quota favored by about two-thirds of the respondents. The split did not seem to parallel pro- or anti-integration lines. Of those who favored the quota, some did so because it would limit the number of blacks and others because it would, they thought, promote integration. Of the opponents, some felt it was discriminatory and others thought that 30 percent was too many blacks.

In public discussion of the quota the split was more even, with the opponents seeming to have a slight edge. Almost all the major Oak Park community groups voted resolutions against the quota, however, and the Community Relations

Commission rejected the quota idea in an eight to seven vote.

Adverse reaction from the metropolitan press was swift, with most of the daily papers and television stations editorializing against the quota proposal. This reaction seemed to take some of the quota's proponents by surprise. They felt that they were being judged unfairly, even labeled as bigots, when they were really trying to achieve a workable program of racial integration.

The image of the community to the outside world was important to Oak Park leaders. They wanted to see the village portrayed as a liberal community striving to make integration work. The notion that Oak Park was a proving ground for integration, with the whole world watching, was expressed time and time again. As one village official said, "We have the chance to become a model city, if we have the guts to become one." Over and over one heard, "If we can't do it in Oak Park, no one can." Said a trustee, "Three years from now, people are going to be coming here to find out what we did." Therefore the media reaction was taken hard and with some appearance of wounded feelings. It was probably a major reason for the ultimate tabling of the quota proposal.

In place of the quota proposal, an extensive, multifaceted integration plan was formulated by one of the trustees. It suggested widespread counseling of home-seekers, possible economic incentives for people to choose homes in locations consistent with integration aims, equity insurance for homeowners, and public relations programs.

To aid in development of the plan, which was at this stage little more than a loose package of potential tactics, the board enlisted the help of the Metropolitan Housing and Planning Council to conduct a "Delphi survey." The Delphi process, developed by the Rand Corporation, is a multistage planning procedure using an anonymously answered questionnaire to tap opinions and determine consensus among experts in a particular field. The core participants were local and regional leaders in housing and related areas of finance and law. They responded to three rounds of questions regarding goals, strategies, tactics, and probable outcomes relevant to racial integration in Oak Park. The fourth and fifth rounds entailed polling a sample of local residents and setting priorities among the planning objectives that had come out of the earlier rounds of the study.

The final Delphi report, which came out in late 1975, firmly supported the policy position that the Board of Trustees had already assumed, by endorsing measures that employed discriminatory treatment based on race for the purpose of preventing resegregation. Among such measures were "affirmative marketing" of east side property to white buyers and setting up a legal case to determine whether racial discrimination for the express purpose of achieving integration would be allowed under federal law. The quota ordinance would have posed such a test. But the quota was left to die, and, though the village attorney was instructed to examine the possibility of a test case, by the end of 1976 no action had been taken that would have forced a clarification of the law in court.

The Delphi process did not yield any new ideas or techniques, but it substantially solidified the village government's stand on integration as a goal and on dispersal as the means. The trustees' enthusiasm for the Delphi process, which had never before been used in planning racial integration, was perhaps due less to its objective results than to what it seemed to stand for: the innovative, sophisticated, rational planning so consistent with the image of the new Oak Park. It exemplified, too, the heightened value being placed on technical expertise in the racial integration strategy.

The village government also continued to strengthen its legislation to maintain housing quality and to tighten enforcement of existing laws. During 1973 the village board had provided for a program of increased apartment inspection. In June 1974 it went a step further and adopted an ordinance requiring the licensing of apartments, with mandatory inspection and a report on the race of occupants required for the annual license renewal. Exteriors of homes were also routinely inspected, and owners were notified by mail of needed repairs. An alley inspector was hired to watch for accumulations of debris, garbage improperly disposed of, illegally parked autos, and anything else that would make the alleys unsightly, unsafe, or unsanitary.

The village government was also seriously exploring the possibility of instituting an "equity assurance" plan to insure homeowners against depreciation of the market values of their homes. It would be a voluntary program, perhaps funded by nominal premiums or by public funds, and would reimburse a claimant for most of the loss he incurred if he sold his home for less than its appraised value. The idea of equity assurance was first developed by a local women's civic group, First Tuesday, then taken over by the village government for further research and planning. By 1977 the plan had been discussed with several private insurance companies, some of which had expressed interest, but all finally declined to underwrite it. It appeared that if the idea were to become workable the village government itself would have to sponsor it; and this ultimately happened, with the program beginning in 1978.

The evolution of the official response to the growing perception of threat of racial change can be summarized in four main points. First, there was expansion of the community relations function, its duties, and its staff. By 1976 the Community Relations Department had a staff of fifteen, a tenfold growth in four years.

Second, there was an elevation of the formal and informal status of community relations workers and of the community relations function within the government hierarchy. An aspect of this was the increasing centralization of control, exemplified by the shift of the major community relations responsibility away from the Community Relations Commission—a citizens' advisory body operating in the legislative sector of government—into the hands of salaried staff who were directly under the supervision of the village manager.

Third, there was an expansion of the mandate assumed by the local government. The local authorities took a broader and broader view of their legitimate concerns and prerogatives. Along with this went an increasing tendency to buttress informal understandings with formal controls. Additional legislation was passed, and measures that had seemed too controversial to take on in 1971 were accepted as commonplace five years later.

Finally, increasing rationalization of the community relations function was evident in its full incorporation into the administrative bureaucracy, in the increasing use of formal controls, and in the replacement of informal local ties by professional expertise as primary personnel qualifications. The use of the Delphi process was, of course, another manifestation and an excellent representation of this trend.

The aim of the village officials had been to act before major problems developed. The extent to which they succeeded is striking when one recalls that in 1973, when community relations and related activity was noticeably stepped up, the suburb was still less than 5 percent black, and no serious problems had surfaced with the real estate and lending industries. For example, when the "for sale" sign ban was passed, a community relations official commented: "There was really nothing going on here. We've been lucky that way. We really haven't had any problems with real estate practices. There was a lot of community pressure for the sign ban. Everyone has their antenna up. People are supersensitive to things they wouldn't have noticed a year ago."

There were two important reasons the community had been sensitized to the point that the village government was able and even compelled to act as early as it did. One was the experience of Austin. Oak Parkers had gotten a close view of the rapid transition of southern Austin and were extremely fearful that the process would be repeated in their own community. Second, the fair housing movement in Oak Park had already brought the issue of race into the political arena at least three years before most people perceived racial change as an imminent threat, and it had helped define Oak Park as an integrated community.[3] That definition, a popular mandate for early action on the issue, and a central authoritative body that was able to act gave Oak Park an advantage Austin lacked.

10

Intervention in Oak Park: Voluntary Organizations

Oak Parkers often described their community as "active," as one with a high level of citizen involvement in community life. Indeed, such voluntary participation won Oak Park the National Municipal League's "All-America City" title (one of ten municipalities so designated throughout the country each year) in 1976. It would be difficult to say, however, that Oak Parkers were on the average more active in civic affairs than their counterparts in neighboring suburbs. As in most suburbs, a majority did not vote in local elections. At even the best-attended civic meetings, only a minute fraction of the populace was represented, and one encountered the same core of community activists at each meeting. Likewise, one found the same handful of people holding memberships or leadership posts in different organizations.

The number of Oak Park residents actively involved in carrying on the business of the community was thus probably not atypically large. What did strike one as atypical was the number and scope of the groups in which these individuals participated. This resulted in a dense organizational web of functionally differentiated components, woven together by multiple overlapping memberships.

Therefore, in contrast to the segmented character of the organizational response to racial change in Austin, the response in Oak Park was mediated through a well-integrated network of groups. While the programs and activities of the major groups tended to dovetail in the overall effort to control racial change, the groups were nevertheless separate organizations, each with its distinct style, set of constraints, and access to resources. This quality of organizational life was an essential key to the effectiveness with which Oak Park dealt with racial change, for the resulting division of labor permitted employment of a range of diverse resources that could not have been tapped by any single organization.

Aside from local government, the organizations most active in the effort to control racial change were the Oak Park Housing Center and the Oak Park Citizens' Action Program, later known as the Oak Park Community Organization. But in addition to these major actors there were also numerous block clubs and some influential neighborhood associations. Furthermore, such diverse groups as businessmen's associations, civic clubs, school organizatons, and a variety of ad hoc groups played important roles from time to time.

It would be impossible to describe all the voluntary group activity relevant to the integration strategy. This chapter therefore focuses on three types of organization: the Housing Center, the Citizens' Action Program, and the block clubs and neighborhood associations. These were selected because their roles were substantial, continuous, and direct and because, different as they were in structure, purpose, and style, they well illustrate the division of labor that was such an important element in managing integration in Oak Park. It is important to remember, nevertheless, that by focusing on these we are omitting from discussion a large number of other organizations whose cumulative influence may have been nearly as great as that of those described. Indeed, it is a central point that whatever the effect of the purposeful activities of these many groups, they fulfilled the essential function of providing a web of communication channels among the community leaders.

The Oak Park
Housing Center

The creation of a housing referral service to "manage" integration in Oak Park by managing the locational choices of its newcomers was largely the work of Roberta Raymond, a longtime
fair housing activist. When the Community Relations Commission failed to respond to the suggestion by the Citizens' Committee for Human Rights, Raymond (who chaired the housing
committee of the latter group) began developing the support
and resources to put the plan into operation privately. The
Housing Center opened in May 1972, with its founder serving
as its director.

A prospectus for the Housing Center issued in January 1972
suggested that the center would fulfill the following purposes:

1. Help attract families from other areas to Oak Park
through the use of brochures, other printed material, newspaper advertising describing the advantages of the community and its heterogeneous nature, and visits to employment centers;
2. Counsel and assist prospective residents who would
benefit by the direct, friendly contact a housing center and its
volunteers would offer;
3. Maintain files regarding the practices of realtors and
lending institutions, as well as the availability of real estate
(both purchase and rentals) in the area;
4. Initiate a continuing community education program on
harmful real estate practices and what residents can do to
fight them;
5. Aid in legal referral for whites and/or blacks who have
experienced discrimination from realtors or lending institutions, and where appropriate, undertake direct action;
6. Provide a forum through which current residents could
meet to exchange ideas and to offer their advice, knowledge
and support.

The budget for the first year was set at $26,500. It was antici-

pated that about one-third of the budget could be met by contributions from local sources, from which $4,000 had been col-
lected in just the first three months of operation. Foundation
grants would be solicited for the remainder. The first major
grant, $8,000 a year for three years from the Wieboldt Founda-
tion, came in October 1972, and it was soon followed by a grant
from CNA Financial for $5,000. As other local and foundation
contributions were added to the coffers, the financing actually
obtained for succeeding years far surpassed the first year's
budget. Annual receipts for 1973 through 1975 fluctuated between $40,000 and $50,000, with approximately half supplied by
foundations and corporations.

The credentials of the center's founder and director included
several years of fair housing activity in the village and a master's degree in sociology. Her energy, drive, and competence
were recognized and respected by other community leaders.
This recognition was a major factor in her ability to win support
for the Housing Center. For example, a member of the village
government's Community Relations Commission, who seemed
initially skeptical of the proposal, had finally conceded, "if the
leadership stays, I have no reservations." She was described by
the director of a metropolitan fair housing group as "the person
with the best feel for what is going on in Oak Park." The support she was able to enlist from prominent elements of the
community should not be underestimated. She had acquired
office space in one of Oak Park's most prestigious and centrally
located churches. Gaining that office was described in a Housing Center brochure as "a minor triumph, for in order to obtain
office space at its present location, the Housing Center had to
win, over a period of months, the support and confidence not
only of the minister and governing boards of the First Congregational Church but of the entire congregation as well." The
village manager said of the Housing Center: "I've put my arms
around it and said, 'Look, I think this is a good thing.' I've
persuaded businessmen to support it financially, which they
have done."

High-level support for the Housing Center extended even to

the local real estate and lending industries. Several local brokers cooperated in supplying listings to the Housing Center. An officer of a local savings and loan institution addressed a letter to local colleagues urging their moral and monetary support of the Housing Center.

Initially, promotion and advertising were the Housing Center's most expensive endeavors (although by 1975 salaries claimed the largest share of the budget, as the Housing Center also became more professional), and these were central functions. Soon after the center opened, a professionally produced sixteen-page brochure, "Oak Park, the People Place," was ready for distribution. The brochure consisted mainly of photographs and short paragraphs on the subjects of "recreation," "convenient transportation," "fine schools," "excellent libraries," "architecture," "activities," "citizen participation," "future plans," and "housing." There was one great difference between this brochure and the kind of publicity that might then have been produced by any of the local real estate firms, and that was the presence of black people in the photographs. Nowhere in the text was integration mentioned except in an allusion to the fair housing ordinance, but the message was there to be interpreted by the reader: Oak Park is a place where blacks, whites, and other races live, work, and get along together. No broker had dared to advertise Oak Park's integration. The Housing Center director had previously urged local brokers to represent Oak Park in their advertising as an integrated community. According to her their uniform response was "Oh, no, we can't do that." The most ambitious professional effort at promoting Oak Park was probably a slide presentation used by one of the firms. There were no blacks to be seen in any of the slides, even in the downtown street scenes, though black people frequently shopped in Oak Park. In fact, as the Housing Center pointed out, there had been "no brochure produced by any village group which sold Oak Park, and, at the same time, pointed out its heterogeneity." The emphasis on integration was more than a reflection of the values held by the leadership. It was of considerable strategic significance, founded on the belief

that long-term neighborhood stability depended upon attracting whites who were seeking integration and not, as sometimes
in the past, fleeing racial change.

The Housing Center placed classified advertisements in a
variety of metropolitan and national media aimed at the young,
white, liberal, upwardly mobile family. The ads were carried in
MS, *Saturday Review,* and the *New Republic* as well as in similarly oriented Chicago-based publications. Brochures and publicity materials were sent out to professional schools and
associations and to major metropolitan employers. The most
ambitious of the Housing Center's public relations efforts
was the commissioning of a feature-length film portraying
the community in its efforts to achieve residential and social
integration among blacks and whites. The local government
later joined the Housing Center as a cosponsor of the film,
which was shown locally and on Chicago television.

The advertising and public relations effort was extremely successful. Almost as soon as the Housing Center opened its doors,
it began receiving more applications for housing than it could
easily handle. Table 15 provides a breakdown by race of the
applicants served and those actually placed by the Housing
Center. The placements remained roughly 90 percent white
throughout the five years covered in the table. The Housing
Center was also successful in distributing white clients
throughout all areas of Oak Park. In fact, as table 16 indicates,
it was able to place more white families in the Hawthorne School
area in southeast Oak Park than in any other neighborhood.
The Housing Center was diligent in its efforts to place white
prospects near the Austin border, while it discouraged blacks
from seeking apartments there. This may partly explain the
substantial dropout rate among black applicants who contacted
the Housing Center but then apparently rented housing
elsewhere or abandoned the search, for the least expensive
housing was most readily available along the Austin border
area. Assuming that, as a group, the black clients had lower
incomes than the white clients, successful attempts to prevent
them from locating in this area could be tantamount to excluding them from the village. Furthermore, the discrimination

blacks were likely to encounter in other parts of the village was not just economic; racial discrimination had not been entirely eliminated from the Oak Park housing market. If the black clients, as a group, also had more children than their white counterparts, as a Housing Center official maintained, they were placed at a further disadvantage.

Table 15	Oak Park Housing Center Applications and Placements, by Race, 1972–76			
	Applicants		Clients Placed	
Period Covered	Black [a]	All Other	Black [a]	All Other
May 1972–August 1973	159	400	—	—
May 1972–May 1973	—	—	30	236
May 1972–December 1973	—	—	49	489
May 1973–April 1974	591	1,566	53	455
May 1974–April 1975	970	2,556	96	893
May 1975–April 1976	1,502	2,835	133	1,094

Source: Oak Park Housing Center Files and Annual Reports, 1973–74; 1974–75; 1975–76.

Note: The time periods used between May 1972 and May 1974 overlap. Different data were available for different periods of time.

[a]Includes interracial couples and families.

The largest single occupational group served by the Housing Center was medical professionals. Oak Park was only a few minutes by el or automobile from Chicago's vast medical center complex. Also within convenient reach were the University of Illinois and the Loyola University School of Medicine. These institutions were important factors in attracting residents to Oak Park, and the Housing Center directed much of its promotion to their students and staff.

Efforts were made to steer white clients to apartments in southeast Oak Park, though they were never denied listings anywhere in the community. At times certain apartments were being "pushed" because they had been vacant for a while or because there was perceived danger of more blacks moving into an area with an existing black concentration. It was important for the Housing Center to demonstrate to landlords along the Austin border area that the Housing Center could place white tenants in their buildings. Racial stabilization depended greatly on landlords in southeast Oak Park finding it profitable to hold vacancies for whites.

Table 16	Oak Park Housing Center Placements, by Race and Location, 1 May 1973–30 April 1974		
	School District	Black/Interracial	All Other
	Beye	7	52
	Emerson	5	100
	Hatch	0	8
	Hawthorne	21	103
	Holmes	0	61
	Irving	3	9
	Lincoln	0	18
	Longfellow	8	43
	Mann	0	11
	Whittier	1	13
	District unknown	8	37
	Total	53	455

Source: Oak Park Housing Center.

The racial characteristics of the neighborhoods to which they were being referred were not usually mentioned to white prospects unless they themselves asked. If blacks were living in the neighborhood, Housing Center volunteers represented it as a stably integrated area into which whites were still moving. Many of the applicants seemed unconcerned about race, and it was difficult to tell if many of them even were aware of the racial mix of the village, though the Housing Center represented the village as integrated in all its promotional material.

Nevertheless, many clients were at least vaguely aware that there were areas of Oak Park with black concentrations. It was not uncommon for applicants to specify "not near Austin," "west Oak Park only," "north Oak Park only," or "not in south Oak Park." It was difficult if not impossible to persuade such people to look at apartments in areas with black concentrations or near the Austin ghetto, but Housing Center staff usually at least challenged their assumptions of the undesirability of the areas. At best, they were sometimes persuaded to reduce the size of their "off-limits" zones. Applicants gave a variety of reasons or no reasons at all for excluding certain areas from consideration. The fears that kept people away from the Austin border were often ones they could not comfortably articulate. When pressed for reasons, people often responded evasively. The resistance of some applicants was nearly impossible to counter because they refused to take responsibility for the decision: for example, "My fiance doesn't want to live near Austin," or "I heard that was a bad neighborhood."

Of course, all the direct observational data on the Housing Center was gathered during the summer of 1972, and at that time the situation was still often described as "touch and go." Confidence in Oak Park's stability seemed to grow with ensuing years.

During the observation period of 1972, client records at the Housing Center were coded by race: "1" for white and "2" for black. Some of the listings, particularly those for apartments within a few blocks of Austin Boulevard and north to about Chicago Avenue, were inscribed, "Do not refer 2s." While the coding system was hardly sophisticated, it did not need to be, since Housing Center staff did not try to conceal the meaning of the code or the nature of the policy.

Occasionally blacks, inadvertently or because they insisted, were sent to view apartments to which the Housing Center was trying to refer only white applicants. One day the superintendent of one of these buildings called the Housing Center to say that two black applicants had come to him that day on referral from the Housing Center and he had turned them away. "Don't send any more blacks here," he said. "We've got eight families already, so don't send any more here." Not long after that, a young black man entered the office to complain that he had been discriminated against at that very building. The director of the Housing Center took him aside and said, "Let me tell you about this building. There are about thirty units, and seven or eight of them are already rented to black families. The landlord is really trying to keep the number down to stabilize the building." After a few minutes of further conversation, the man left the office, seemingly satisfied with the explanation and in agreement with the policy. What had taken place was quite illustrative of that policy, as stated by the director: "We will not send blacks to south Austin Boulevard. We tell them that and tell them why. We are very careful to explain in detail why we will not."

At the same time, the director pointed out, all clients had a right to view any apartment listed, and though clients were counseled in accordance with the village's official policy on dispersal and referred to the Community Relations Department for further counseling, all were free in the end to apply for any available housing unit.

While ticklish situations were usually met forthrightly by the director, some of the volunteer staff had more difficulty in dealing so candidly with the applicants, and they were more likely to employ tactful dodges when asked embarrassing questions such as what the codes stood for. Such expedient evasions were, however, contrary to Housing Center policy. The operation of the Housing Center was sensitive business at best, involving as it did differential treatment of blacks and whites, and any hint of subterfuge could only lead it into greater legal jeopardy. Eventually the need to make the policy open, clear, and explicit was met by distributing to each client a three-by-five card with a brief statement of Housing Center policy:

> The policy of the Oak Park Housing Center is to assist in stabilizing integration in the village. To this end, there will be encouragement of white clients to move into buildings or areas that are already integrated, and the encouragement of black clients to move into buildings or areas which are not substantially integrated. Listings will be provided in keeping with this policy, with the understanding that under both local and federal laws, all clients are free to pursue the housing of their choice.

Clients were not the only ones who were apt to raise problems by their misperceptions of the Housing Center's policy and role. Even after a full year of operation and extensive local publicity, the purpose of the Housing Center was not well understood by many small landlords—for instance, those renting half of a two-flat—whose participation in the real estate business was infrequent and nonprofessional. Contact with such landlords most frequently came about when the Housing Center checked *Oak Leaves* classifieds or attempted to refer clients to apartments advertised there. A Housing Center client told the following story at the center office, much to the relish of himself and the office staff:

> Did Bobbie tell you about that woman she called for an apartment for me? It was on Austin. The woman said, "Is he colored?" Bobbie said, "Well, he's sort of white with a little pink." The woman said, "Is he *colored*?" Bobbie said "No, as a matter of fact, he's caucasian," and the woman said, "Well, we don't want any of those either."

Another landlady told the staff member who called to verify information on an apartment advertised in the paper, "This is a family thing, and we prefer to rent it privately." One can only surmise what she meant by that, since she had advertised the apartment in the newspaper. Others simply refused to cooperate, making such remarks as "I'm not interested" or "I've got enough applicants already." Anticipating such rebuffs, some of the volunteer staff did not identify themselves as from the Housing Center. However, the director said that she always identified herself and encouraged the staff to do so as well. One volunteer hung up after a call, saying, "Boy, she doesn't like the Housing Center a bit. Remember not to call that one." The director replied, "When I get ones like that, I tell them I'll be happy to refer them to about seventeen satisfied landlords," referring to those owners or managers of large buildings who at that time were routinely listing their vacancies with the Housing Center.

The importance of the Housing Center derived from the functions it performed relative to the local real estate market. These were functions that were called for by the inception of racial change in the community but were performed poorly, if at all, by the normal real estate practitioners.

First, the Housing Center became a unique promoter and agent for Oak Park's real estate. A racially integrated suburb may be considered a suburb with a specialized ecological function, not at all the same as the all-white suburb. Those backing the Housing Center recognized that if Oak Park were integrated, its residential role would be altered. In other words, a new market would have to be exploited. Without intervention Oak Park also seemed destined to change its role, but by becoming a receiver of blacks exclusively. The word had to go out, through effective advertising and promotion, to those whites who would be attracted to a racially integrated residential environment. Brokers had refused to recognize the changing role and the changing market. For them to undertake the task of exploiting this new market would have meant running counter to the grain of a conservative business ethic, restructuring their sales efforts, designing radically altered advertising programs, and, all told, navigating in uncharted and altogether risky waters.

Second, the Housing Center provided coordination that was practically nonexistent in th rental market. Having a large number of rental listings at all times enabled the Housing Center to practice "reverse steering" by directing whites to southeast Oak Park and blacks to all other sectors. In the course of its operations, the Housing Center was able to monitor who moved where. It exchanged information with the Community Relations Department so that, at least until 1973, each agency had an up-to-date map of the location of black residents. This information was required to make the reverse steering procedure rational. The combination of record-keeping and direct participation in the real estate market was a Housing Center function that was not duplicated by any other village agency or organization, although passage of the apartment licensing law did allow the village government again to keep accurate records of the race of residents by location.

Third, the Housing Center served as a watchdog over real estate and lending practices. Applicants for housing continually fed the Housing Center information on apartment upkeep and racial discrimination in rentals. Several racial discrimination suits were filed in federal court as a result of information supplied through the Housing Center.

Fourth, the Housing Center provided a central point for exchanging and disseminating pertinent information and for catalyzing new strategies to promote racial stability. When there was difficulty in selling homes to whites in southeast Oak Park, the Housing Center, through its director, took a direct role in creating a partnership to buy homes that came on the market there. In 1973 three homes were owned by the partners and were being rented to white families. A similar venture involved the purchase and renovation of deteriorating apartment buildings in southeast Oak Park. In 1973 one such building had been purchased and renovated, apartments were being rented to both blacks and whites, and the building remained integrated and apparently stable in succeeding years.

There are different perspectives from which the relative success of the Housing Center—or any organization—can be evaluated. Two important aspects of organizations that can be rated in this way are the viability or survival potential of the organization and the extent to which organizational goals are met.

The Oak Park Housing Center had to be judged remarkably successful in establishing itself as a viable and even powerful organization in the community. It had gained and maintained support from the active segment of the community. It had been editorially endorsed in the local press more than once, and it had received publicity through news stories and feature articles in the local and metropolitan press that could hardly have been more laudatory had they been the Housing Center's own publicity releases. Manpower had been at least sufficient to handle continuously growing numbers of clients, and financial resources had grown steadily. The local government authorities, once they overcame their initial trepidation, treated the Housing Center almost as an official arm. The Housing Center report became a routine feature of Community Relations Commission meetings, and the advice and opinion of Housing Center leaders was solicited in much the same way that village department heads were asked for their expert information in the policy-making process. It took less than a year for the Housing Center to assume a position very near the top of the prestige hierarchy of community and civic organizations.

The Housing Center began receiving national recognition in 1976 by being one of the three volunteer projects that qualified Oak Park for the "All-America City" award. In 1977 the Housing Center itself won two more awards, the Chicago Community Trust's "James Brown IV Award for Outstanding Community Service," and a Fair Housing Award from the United States Department of Housing and Urban Development.

The effectiveness with which the Housing Center moved toward its major goals is partly implied in the data regarding placements summarized earlier in tables 15 and 16. The Housing Center was able to attract white families and to place them at least within the school districts with increasing black population concentrations. The ratio of white to black placements aided by the Housing Center remained stable, even though the proportion of black applicants increased. In terms of its immediate aims, the Housing Center had to be judged a success.

There were external factors operating in the Housing Center's favor that have been touched on already. First, the cheapest housing in Oak Park was along the Austin border. As long as the Housing Center successfully counseled blacks away from there, the income level of blacks entering Oak Park through the Housing Center was maintained at a higher level, and the total number coming in was probably reduced. This factor, of course, promotes racial balance only if whites can be placed in vacancies in the area. If the landlords could not get enough white renters, the low cost of the housing near the front of the ghetto expansion would likely accelerate change.

A second external factor made it easier to place whites in vacancies in southeast Oak Park—the proximity of the schools and hospitals mentioned earlier. They brought to Oak Park a group of young professionals and students in need of cheap housing. The director attributed the Housing Center's ability to draw whites to southeast Oak Park to the low cost of apartments there: "It's an economic thing, mostly. If whites are looking for an apartment in the $145 range, it's going to be Austin Boulevard." In addition to the economic factor, the transience of the students might also make them more willing than others to move into an area that might be resegregating.

This transient nature of many of the whites moving into southeast Oak Park bothered some residents of longer standing. They felt the area could not be stabilized unless whites with a more enduring commitment could be attracted. It seems quite possible, however, that the schools and hospitals could provide continuous white replacement, in spite of the transience of the individuals, though the character of the community would be changed, even if its racial composition was not. Many longtime Oak Parkers resisted facing the fact that racial stabilization of the village would inevitably require or result in other changes in the physical, social, and demographic character of the community.

Citizens' Action
Program

The most active grass-roots group was the Oak Park Citizens' Action Program (CAP), which began as the local affiliate of the Chicago Metropolitan Citizens' Action Program (Metro CAP). Metro CAP was originally an antipollution organization. Having won significant support and publicity on that issue, it broadened its scope to include action on any issue relevant to the local citizenry.

As Metro CAP widened its range of concerns, Oak Park CAP did the same, directing its attention almost exclusively to local community issues and eventually severing its ties with the parent group, changing its name in 1974 to Oak Park Community Organization (OPCO). To avoid confusion and because the research reported here was for the most part conducted before the name change, I will refer to the group as CAP. Even before it was renamed, CAP's priorities were local ones, and the change in name simply reflected the program it had already undertaken.

CAP operated on a very small budget of, at best, a few thousand dollars a year, which came from dues, modest contributions, and special fund-raising events. Except for a meagerly paid organizer who had originally been assigned by Metro CAP, CAP relied on volunteer manpower. In later years the group did not even have the part-time organizer.

In May 1973 CAP had fifty-five paid members, of which about forty were active in the organization. In addition, CAP claimed between two hundred and three hundred "sympathetic supporters and contributors . . . depending upon the issue involved." CAP strove for broad-based, grass-roots representation. One of its leaflets stated:

> CAP does not represent any one neighborhood, political philosophy, or socio-economic class . . . .
> CAP citizen support cuts across neighborhood, political, religious, and socio-economic lines.

In the strict sense, these claims were valid. CAP did draw support from that wide range of people—but not proportionately. CAP members and supporters tended to be of a broad age range and largely represented the middle of the middle class. They were mostly white, but the small number of black supporters was at least proportionate to the small black population in Oak Park. They were likely to be of a liberal political bent. More than two-thirds of the 1973 members lived in the southern half of Oak Park, and only two lived in the northwest quarter. A CAP leader commented on the lack of proportional representation and hazarded some guesses as to the reasons:

> Some areas are not well represented. I don't think we have a single CAP member in the northwest section of Oak Park. That's a pretty affluent area, so they're probably not worried. I have been concentrating in the southeast and have good connections there . . . . Most of our membership seems to be fairly liberal. That's unfortunate. Of course we don't want to exclude liberals from participating, but we need more conservative members if we're going to have cross-sectional representation. Maybe liberals are just the kind of people who get "elected" in Oak Park.

In its literature, CAP described itself as an "independent, non-partisan group of Oak Park residents dedicated to action on village issues . . . . CAP members set the organization's goals." This is somewhat misleading on two counts. On one hand, the issue goal-selection procedure tended to conform to the usual pattern of organizational oligarchy. The executive committee actually selected issues and goals and called meetings for their presentation, discussion, and routine ratification. Meetings were not held on a regular schedule, but were called whenever the executive committee felt the need. On the other hand, CAP was forced by its desire for broad-based support to be democratic in program content. This meant that the issues selected had to appeal to a target constituency broader than its actual membership, and CAP leaders thus went beyond the CAP membership to draw ideas for their "action issues."

The issues CAP acted on were varied, but they naturally tended to revolve around the racial stabilization of the community, as most issues did in Oak Park after 1971. There were three implicit criteria for specific issues and goals: they had to be of broad appeal, they had to be newsworthy enough to generate local press coverage, and they had to have a reasonable chance of success. CAP's limited resources made selecting the right issues even more crucial. For example, a CAP leader described CAP's posture on the race issue and indicated some of the attendant difficulties:

> We're not trying to keep blacks out of Oak Park, but on the other hand we're not trying to bring blacks into Oak Park either. We're neither integrationist nor segregationist. Neither type of group could get broad support here. We have some blacks working with us. Maybe you know [name]. She's a new black resident who's been working with us. We've had people come up after meetings and say, "If you people had been around earlier, we could have kept those niggers out." And this after the same meetings where blacks like her were present! It's very delicate. It's difficult to find issues where we can get this kind of broad support.

With no direct community decision-making power of its own, CAP's role in affecting community decisions was limited to the pressure it could bring to bear upon agents who had that authority. Therefore CAP's success in attaining any particular goal and in maintaining its own viability over time was very largely dependent on the quantity and nature of the support it could muster. To be an effective pressure group, CAP needed to be able to assert with credibility that its resident support was both substantial and representative of the community.

Straight news coverage of CAP actions and issues was an indispensable publicity resource. The group generally fared well in the local press. Although leaders occasionally complained of lack of coverage of specific events, CAP activities were often extensively covered in the news pages. One local paper ran a moderately critical editorial questioning CAP's motives in one of its campaigns, but in general CAP was editorially ignored, although the newspapers took various positions on the issues it tackled.

Finally, CAP had to choose program goals it had a good chance of attaining, if it were not to suffer the attrition likely to follow continual defeats. Thus even apparent defeats were apt to be interpreted as partial victories, as when CAP failed to block village approval of a high-rise apartment development but took credit for lowering its proposed height. CAP's potential effectiveness was based on a cyclical process in which each win could generate increased support and thus raise the probability of a victory on the next issue. Repeated victories were an important ingredient of the "bandwagon effect" CAP hoped for. When more than a hundred residents turned up at a local savings and loan office to demonstrate their support for CAP's demand for an antiredlining pledge from the firm's management, the crowd size surpassed CAP leaders' expectations. A participant said to the CAP organizer, "If you get an agreement tonight, you'll have two hundred at the next one." The organizer agreed.

The issue- and goal-selection criteria were evident in some of the issues and policies CAP rejected. It steered clear of issues that were highly controversial or divisive and positions that might have been considered too extreme. CAP fought the proposed downtown high rise, but it refused—to the chagrin of some of its members and supporters—to reject in principle any high-rise development for Oak Park. Such a position would have been not only extreme, but probably futile, given the obvious commitment of Oak Park's business, political, and civic leaders to physical and economic redevelopment of the community. Similarly, CAP took the "safe" position of condemning redlining without condemning FHA and VA mortgages in the village generally, although some members urged it to do so. CAP leaders reiterated, "We are not against FHA mortgages per se." The bitterness an anti-FHA position might have engendered became very clear at a CAP meeting when a young woman responded with an angry and almost tearful tirade to another member's suggestion that anyone too poor to get a conventional mortgage was too poor to maintain an Oak Park home. The woman took the remark as a personal affront, since she and her husband had purchased their home with a low down payment and a federally insured mortgage. Furthermore, the anti-FHA positions taken by some Chicago-area groups had been widely interpreted as antiblack.

CAP also rejected issues it felt were of low concern or possibly futile. When CAP was asked to participate in a campaign launched by a local woman to reduce swimming pool fees, the CAP executive committee turned down the request. The woman was allowed to make a presentation to the general membership, but she was scheduled at the end of an already full agenda. The chairman then pointed out that any discussion or consideration of her plan was precluded because the park district recreation hall where they were meeting had to be cleared in ten minutes. He informed those attending that the executive committee did not recommend adopting the issue and suggested that individual CAP members work with the woman on an ad hoc committee. Then, if it looked as if it were a "going issue," CAP might get involved as a group. It was clear from his remarks that CAP leaders had failed to endorse the issue because they feared it had low appeal and little chance of success. (The campaign, as a matter of fact, did ultimately succeed.) By controlling the agenda, leaders were able to prevent the membership from going over their heads to take up issues that leaders apparently felt would be a waste of resources.

On the other hand, it is useful to note the issues CAP did get involved in. CAP opposed the construction of a twin-tower apartment building, as mentioned before. The village government approved the development and made the requisite zoning changes, but CAP took credit for scaling down the project from fifty-four to thirty-seven stories. CAP pressured the village government to pass the ordinance banning "for sale" and "sold" signs from residential property. It demanded increased police patrolling and provision in the budget for thirty-six additional officers. It also advocated relaxing some of the police recruitment criteria so as to increase the pool of applicants and decrease recruitment time. The police department agreed to allot more patrols to southeast Oak Park, using off-duty police to supply the extra manpower, and the village board agreed to provide for more policemen in the budget though not to change the recruitment policies.

CAP supported increased inspection of apartments for code violations. An ordinance was passed to allow for random inspection of housing units as well as for inspection upon complaint. In 1974 an even more extensive measure was passed, requiring licensing of apartment buildings.

CAP asked that the village government, through the Community Relations Commission or the Community Relations Department, assume the task, which CAP itself had been performing, of monitoring local real estate and lending practices through systematic, covert "testing." The Community Relations Commission voted unanimously to take over the responsibility, and the village board reluctantly gave its approval when it appeared that refusal would result in a major split between the trustees and the commission.

There were few community issues that were beyond CAP's scope, provided they met the criteria of salience and some probability of success. However, CAP's highest priority became the issue of redlining.

CAP's campaign against mortgage disinvestment in Oak Park began with the local lenders. It applied direct pressure on them, through media publicity, to prove through public release of records that mortgages were not being restricted in any part of Oak Park. CAP also lobbied for a provision in the fair housing ordinance that would explicitly outlaw redlining. The local lenders responded to CAP pressure by forming an organization called Financial Institutions Special Committee on Area Leadership (FISCAL), which included all four of Oak Park's banks and four of its savings and loan companies. FISCAL members agreed to publish the number and dollar amounts of conventional, FHA, and VA mortgages by quadrant of the village. The village government drafted an antiredlining amendment and scheduled a vote on it. In the meantime, it was rumored that the trustees planned to table the measure. CAP waged a last-minute telephone campaign to get residents out to the village board meeting. The campaign was successful in attracting a large crowd to the meeting in support of the ordinance, and it passed.

After its local antiredlining successes, CAP began to reach beyond Oak Park to attack redlining by major downtown Chicago firms. It allied itself with wider Chicago area groups to apply pressure on the large institutions whose policies affected the entire metropolitan region, on HUD agencies, on the banking industry's regulatory boards, and on the appropriate state and federal legislative committees. One of the groups with which CAP (by this time operating as OPCO) frequently acted in concert was the Metropolitan Area Housing Alliance (MAHA), a group that had become very effective in training and placing community organizers and in applying leverage for change in housing policies and practices at higher political levels. The Illinoios state redlining law, for example, was largely spurred by MAHA efforts. MAHA had been founded by former leaders of Austin's OBA, and their experience in Austin was used as the explicit model for community organization and organizer training.

On its home territory at least, however, CAP was as discreet in choosing its tactics as it was in selecting issues and formulating policy. In this respect it differed from its progenitor, Metro CAP, which readily used direct confrontation. The philosophy of Metro CAP was inspired by the late Saul Alinsky, but Oak Park CAP tended to shun the Alinskyite label, which for many people was synonymous with radicalism. A CAP leader was quoted as explaining, "Whether to be noisy depends on whether it will do any good to get a decision made or action taken."[1] Such justification of the means by the end may be a hallmark of the Alinsky method, but in Oak Park the means were seldom especially noisy. CAP usually worked through channels. The most aggressive confrontation CAP made against a local target was a demonstration in the lobby of the savings and loan firm it had accused of redlining. In that instance the quiet, well-dressed, well-mannered, and overwhelmingly average-looking crowd of about a hundred Oak Parkers, standing around and chatting amiably with one another, bore not the vaguest resemblance to the chanting and shouting Metro CAP protesters who were often seen on the television news. One CAP leader was clearly annoyed when I compared CAP with the Organization for a Better Austin. "I'm sure there must be some similarities," he replied, sounding as if he could not imagine what those similarities might be, "but certainly we're different in style."

Even using utmost caution and discretion, by its very nature and purpose CAP was bound to arouse some suspicion and even hostility. It received covert support and modest financial contributions from some individuals who felt that, for business or political reasons, they could not be identified as CAP members. Local government officials handled CAP gingerly. For them the organization was sometimes very useful, sometimes exceedingly bothersome, and always potentially dangerous. A community relations staff member said of his group's relations with CAP:

> We try to cooperate with them. It's sort of sticky. We support their general goal, but we don't always support their tactics. What if it came out in *Oak Leaves* that the commission had passed a resolution supporting them—and then the next week they might be off on some extreme tangent.

In the savings and loan dispute, a community relations official had been the mediator between CAP and the firm. When CAP planned the demonstration at the savings and loan office, the official made an abortive attempt to defuse the situation by changing the meeting place to the village hall. Angry CAP leaders, who had not been consulted in advance, vetoed the plan, and one of them said of the community relations official, "He's all for community participation, but he gets very nervous when it takes place."

Because CAP was forced to adhere to its own criteria in selecting issues and goals, alliances with other groups could take place only on an issue-by-issue basis. This may have caused some resentment from other organizations that felt CAP used them for its own purposes. Furthermore, CAP's need for newspaper coverage left it vulnerable to charges of "headline hunting." A high local official made these observations:

> There is evidence of conflict between the Hawthorne and Beye neighborhood organizations and CAP. Those organizations grew directly out of the schools and their immediate areas, and their concerns are for their immediate communities. They have a different set of agenda items than CAP. Also, CAP is the sort of organization that engages in headline seeking. They have to. It's important for them to get publicity. If one is cynical, one might say that they are only out to get publicity, but I don't hold to that position myself.

However, the same official later said of CAP, "Their track record isn't very good," explaining that they had lost on the high-rise issue and that they were prone to take credit on other issues that was not really due them: "The "for sale" sign ban had been in the works before CAP took notice of it. Then CAP jumped in and took credit when it was passed. That tells you something about them. That tells you something."

Opposition from some quarters was predictable, of course. When I asked the president of the real estate board about CAP's campaign against redlining, he replied, "Ridiculous! That was overexaggerated for people to get their names in the paper."

Despite some critics' attempts to cast CAP in the role of a rather noisy but otherwise insignificant minority, the group did not become isolated from the community's mainstream. It is true that recognition by ordinary residents was not particularly high, despite the amount of local press coverage given to CAP activities. (A CAP volunteer soliciting donations in the neighborhoods conceded that most of the people did not know about the organization: "They hear 'CAP' and most of them think it's just another organization asking for money, like the Red Cross or Community Chest.") But CAP drew support from the small but important segment of the community who were actively involved in the suburb's affairs. Sympathizers, who could often be counted on to back various issues, included people who were very well integrated into Oak Park's social and political network: village commission members, pastors of large churches, and so on. Although CAP's constituency consisted largely of people who probably would have been involved in the same issues even if CAP had not existed, the group functioned as an important catalyst and instrument for that activity. It occupied a distinct niche in the network of organizations and institutions responding to the prospect of racial change in Oak Park.

Block Clubs

Block clubs, called Hundred Clubs, were established by the village government in 1968 under the auspices of the Village Beautification Commission. The village was divided into fourteen geographical areas, each with a Hundred Club area chairman. The area chairmen had "neighborhood assistants," and, ideally, each block had a block chairman.

The local government intended that the Hundred Clubs would strengthen the mechanisms of informal social control and lead to improved maintenance of homes and property, a vital concern because of the age of the village's housing. They were further expected to foster neighborhood cohesion and to provide channels of communication between government and citizenry. While the communication was in theory two-way, it was of more interest to local officials that they had a readily available forum for disseminating information to residents. As such the block clubs provided inexpensive, wide coverage.

In 1972 four hundred of Oak Park's approximately five hundred blocks were officially organized as Hundred Clubs. Many, however, were dormant. As would be expected, the greatest stimulus to block club activity was the perception of threat—notably threat of racial change, although such events as

unpopular zoning changes also provoked at least temporary
flurries of activity. As the perception of imminent racial change
grew, the southeast block clubs became by far the most active in
the village. They met frequently and elicited considerable time
and effort from some of their members. They also assumed the
right to shape and schedule their own goals and priorities, as
opposed to passively accepting the agenda suggested by their
official government sponsor. This meant that they sometimes
acted as opposition groups to local government, presenting officials with their grievances and demands. The southeast block
clubs became extremely suspicious for a time that they were
being "written off" by the village government. The creation of a
"historic preservation district" in north Oak Park at about the
same time that suggestions were being made for a large-scale
urban renewal project along Oak Park's eastern border led to
allegations of "preservation for the north, urban renewal for the
south."

The shifting role and agenda of the block clubs were not
wholly unwelcome to the village government. Official recognition of this shift was given when the administration of the
Hundred Clubs was transferred to the Community Relations
Department when it was formed in 1972. Even when the
Hundred Clubs functioned as pressure groups, they could be
useful to the government in justifying policy decisions to other
segments of the community. A good example was the ban on
"for sale" signs. When the block clubs turned their pressure on
the brokers and lenders, they were exercising leverage that government officials could covertly applaud but could not use
themselves.

The Hundred Clubs were in an especially advantageous position in that their legitimacy, or right to represent, was not
questioned by those in authority. This was one of their greatest
resources. There were two reasons they held this position. First,
the village government was in no position to repudiate its own
creation. Technically, Hundred Clubs were organs of the village
government. Second, the village gave high priority in its official
and public ideology to "grass-roots" participation. Officials
frequently used the term "grass roots" to describe the Hundred

Clubs' programs and activities, seldom applying that label to any other community organization. The Hundred Clubs were the officially designated grass roots, upon which the government bestowed its blessings. Thus they were absolutely free from the need to spend resources, as CAP, OBA, THA, and similar groups did, in defending their claim to be representative.

The emphasis on grass-roots action deserves some further comment. It might be popular and useful for any local government to claim grass-roots involvement. Oak Park departed from the norm in the extent to which this aspect of democratic ideology was emphasized, encouraged, and frequently allowed to affect policy decisions. In what was defined as a potential crisis situation, the local government needed to maintain and reinforce its own base of support and consensus, on the one hand, and to reinforce resident identification with the community on the other. The grass-roots ideology, operating through the Hundred Clubs, filled the bill in both respects. It would lend the government the legitimacy of "participatory democracy," and it might also be expected to enhance the value of the local neighborhood for its residents, through physical improvement and increased neighboring. Furthermore, to the extent that it involved local residents in planning and organization and other time- and energy-consuming tasks, their investments in the community were increased. Presumably, this would render them less apt to withdraw.

A severe limitation on the effectiveness of the Hundred Clubs was scale. They attempted to overcome this by joining together to form larger neighborhood organizations or by creating formal communication channels among blocks—newsletters, for instance. One neighborhood organization, composed of individual block clubs, was operating in northeast Oak Park in 1973. In southeast Oak Park a monthly newsletter was being published and the Hawthorne and Beye neighborhood councils, named after the areas' elementary schools, had been formed. Such larger territorial coalitions of block clubs developed independently of and with little apparent relation to the official geographical area groupings of the Hundred Clubs.

The Hundred Clubs and the neighborhood councils also entered into temporary issue-based alliances with other independent village organizations such as CAP.

Although the block clubs were founded by an external and superordinate group—that is, the village government—this body could in no way control or determine their growth and development, either ideologically or organizationally. Rather, the block clubs evolved in response to indigenously perceived interests, needs, and goals. In this evolution they went from dormancy to gradually escalating activity, they developed autonomy of purpose and operation and functional independence from their parent body, and they followed up this new autonomy by reconstituting themselves into larger groups and coalitions as suited their self-determined needs.

Interorganizational
Relations

Unlike those in Austin, interorganizational relations in Oak Park were generally harmonious. There were, to be sure, numerous occasions for conflict, stemming from the diverse characters of the organizations and their particular ideologies, needs, and goals. Conflict also followed quite naturally from intensification of the effort toward racial stabilization. But the conflict was kept under control by community actors who took care to discourage divisive internecine battles either within or among organizations.

In Oak Park the bargaining for a share of control over the housing market was carried on with the assumption of basic consensus, shared values, and shared ultimate goals. This was not so much a naive belief in the mutual goodwill of the participants as it was their provisional agreement on ground rules. While this tacit consensus masked real underlying conflicts that were sometimes laid bare, in the long run it held together and provided a relatively effective framework for common action.

The consensual climate was at once apparent in the general tone of the public and organizational meetings: reserved, orderly, with spontaneity confined within the bounds of a tacitly accepted script. I was continually struck by the way speakers could voice apparently acrimonious tirades, then conclude with compliments to the village board, commission, or whatever body had convened the meeting for its honesty, integrity, industry, and so on. For example, a representative of the Oak Park–River Forest Citizens' Committee for Human Rights launched a loud and vehement oral attack on the Community Relations Commission at one of the commission meetings, accusing it of timidity, lethargy, and lack of initiative or creativity. All the same, there was a sense that such things were being spoken among friends. Everyone was on a first-name basis, and the speech was concluded with the enthusiastic and apparently sincere compliment, "You're a great group!" Then, turning to the commission's administrator, the speaker continued, "We love you. We think the job you're doing is magnificent." This was not an isolated incident but an example of something observed over and over. The abrupt shifting of gears could leave one bewildered until one recognized, after seeing some repetition of the pattern, that in Oak Park public conflict was normally contained within certain bounds that were well known to the active participants. They were seldom violated by the usual activists, the "joiners" who made the rounds from organization to organization and from one meeting to another. The exceptions were often residents who were not normally involved in civic affairs but were out because a particular issue or incident had aroused their anger.

The question arises whether such affirmations of mutual trust and goodwill were mere tactical ploys. To some extent no doubt they were, but not entirely. A basic ingredient of the political environment in Oak Park was, after all, a trust in the local leaders, who were seen not as politicians, but as fellow residents accepting their civic responsibilities. Furthermore, active citizens in Oak Park were mostly secure, middle-class professional and business people. Having trust in local officials, as well as in the local real estate and lending people, was a matter of having trust in members of one's own group—in one's peers.

This assumption of consensus may be best seen in times of conflict. In such times the normally latent assumption becomes manifest in the attempts to maintain or restore it. This was exemplified by the dealings between the real estate industry and the local authorities. Even the local real estate and lending professionals were within the circle of shared values. Their place was protected by other community leaders, who carefully stressed the distinction between the "locals" and the "outsiders." Oak Park leaders took the converse of OBA's rule of thumb: in Oak Park the local brokers and lenders were friends until they proved themselves enemies.

One of the important specific justifications local authorities often used for passing measures unpopular with the real estate industry was that they felt the local real estate board could not control the outside brokers. That it could and would effectively control local brokers was tacitly taken for granted. That all local participants were members of the same in-group, with the outsiders as potential threats, was the prevailing definition, and care was taken to maintain it.

If the local brokers were to be accorded that place in the in-group, however, some responsive gesture was expected from them to validate the trust that had been extended. For example, the local real estate board was asked late in 1971 to come up with a voluntary plan for limiting signs. By the early part of 1972 the Community Relations Commission grew impatient because no formal plan had been produced. There were insinuations of "foot-dragging," and some commission members favored immediate drafting of an ordinance against the "for sale" signs. Before that was done, however, there was a lengthy and heated exchange between the commission and the president of the real estate board over the guiding principle of conduct adhered to by local real estate men. In a discussion that became increasingly hostile on both sides, the commissioners tried to persuade the real estate board president to give at least lip service to the thesis that the primary concern should be the welfare of the community or, as it was put several times, "human sensitivities." The board president, however, refused to talk in terms other than what constituted good or bad merchandising techniques. His responsibility, he was saying, was to the principles of the profession and nothing else, although he repeatedly denied that there could be any conflict between professional interests and the welfare of the local community. The commission seemed to want a verbal recognition that they were all playing the same game. The board president's refusal to give this may have ended any chance to avoid mandatory controls. The conflict was not resolved to mutual satisfaction. But the time spent on the point, and the fact that commission members and the real estate board president alluded over and over to their disappointment in one another, gave a clue to their assumption that consensus should have been attainable.

The brokers also sought verbal assurance from the village authorities. Many brokers felt they had very little freedom in the conduct of their business as it related to minorities and very little power in local affairs. The village government was informally asking them to practice reverse steering. Brokers complained that this would be in violation of federal law. Some of them called for the village board to pass a resolution backing them up—that is, acknowledging that by reverse steering they would be adhering to official village policy. At that time the village government was not ready to take such an open step. But again the assumption seemed to be that all parties were oriented to the same ultimate ends and that with mutual give and take, conflicts could be overridden.

Even CAP, in its campaign to get local lending firms to sign antiredlining pledges, played down as much as possible any inherent or necessary conflicts between the goals of the firms and the interests of the local community. CAP officers emphasized that when the pledges were obtained, they would be exploited for the best possible publicity both for the lending firms and for CAP. This was described by a CAP officer as "the gentle approach: good press for us and good press for the savings and loans."

Because the various groups in Oak Park had very different capabilities and constraints, and because there was basic agreement on the ultimate goals, a high degree of structural integration was able to develop among them. Joint ventures were commonplace, as when CAP and the Hundred Clubs joined forces to combat alleged real estate steering. Sometimes a group wanted a task accomplished that it could not do but another group could. The Housing Center and the Community Relations Department together sponsored an educational seminar on promoting Oak Park for real estate personnel and community volunteers. It had been a Housing Center idea, but government sponsorship gave it an "official" quality that made its success more probable, especially by rendering it more palatable to the real estate brokers, some of whom still distrusted the Housing Center. When the Community Relations Department was legally precluded from applying for township revenue-sharing funds for one of its programs, it passed the program over to a local civic group to represent as its own. (The funds were not forthcoming, however, possibly because the ploy was disclosed by other local leaders who thought it highly unethical.) When problems were anticipated from one particular real estate firm, a Housing Center representative said that if the broker caused any problems, "we'll just get rid of him." When I asked how this could be done, the reply was, "There are ways. You just have to talk to the right people. CAP would love to get its hands on something like this."

A pattern of specialization developed, with each group contributing to the total effort in ways for which it was inherently best suited—the village government for legal regulation and deployment of large-scale resources within the constraints of acceptability to the community; CAP for pressure tactics that few of the other groups felt free to employ; the Housing Center for extralegal manipulation of the housing market; the block clubs for mobilization at the grass-roots level; and so forth.

This well-integrated, interdependent pattern was greatly aided by the overlapping roles and multiple group memberships of the participants. Active members of CAP did volunteer work at the Housing Center. On the Housing Center board were members of the other important local organizations. The League of Women Voters and First Tuesday, another women's civic group, were well represented on village commissions, either by the members themselves or by their husbands, and the women also were often CAP members and Housing Center volunteers. Some overlap of roles was deliberate policy. It had been the practice of the village board, for instance, to make appointments to the Community Relations Commission according to functional sector. Informally, therefore, there was a lending industry seat, a broker's seat, a school board or faculty seat, a black seat, a southeast Oak Park seat, and so on.

The overlapping networks of affiliations of individual leaders and activists were important channels for informal communication and pressure. To a great extent, communication and cooperation between groups were accomplished through people who occupied positions in each.

The role of the village government in maintaining this complicated web of groups, individuals, and interests can hardly be overestimated. An absolutely crucial fact was that in Oak Park the village government was the center through which the overall racial stabilization effort was coordinated. Often keeping a relatively low profile itself, especially during the early years of the effort, the village government could delegate to other groups the tasks it dared not or, legally, could not undertake. Because it stayed within the bounds of community acceptability, it could function as an arbitrator and mediator among the other participants. Village officials used their influence, for example, to arrange meetings between CAP and the lenders and between the Housing Center and the real estate board. The result was a degree of horizontal organization and integration that was lacking in Austin.[2] Umbrella groups, which OBA and THA both were, are supposed to provide such horizontal links; but insofar as they also undertake direct action strategies and tactics against other local interests and institutions, they undermine their legitimacy with some segments of the community and therefore also undermine their effectiveness as coordinators. THA maintained moral legitimacy and acceptance by important segments of the community—businessmen, politicians, and so forth—at the cost of not being able to deal with the thorny issues at hand, such as real estate practices or slumlords. OBA, on the other hand, through its confrontational tactics was able to wield considerable power against the institutions, but it had to win every victory on its own, without long-range compromise and without the voluntary cooperation of influential people and groups. It had to use controversy to raise a necessary level of citizen support, and this made it difficult to bargain with particular institutions once the citizenry had been mobilized.[3]

As we have seen, intervention strategies by community organizations and institutions were very similar in content in Oak Park and Austin. The real difference lay in the number, type, and range of groups that put those strategies into effect. In Oak Park, the outcome of a division of labor among more or less specialized, differentiated groups was a more extensive actualization of potential resources, greater efficiency, and greater overall effectiveness. It also meant that conflicts could occur between groups without becoming total wars that would immobilize the entire organizational structure.

In Austin, on the other hand, the organizational structure was sharply segmented. Two mutually exclusive groups dominated community action. The Town Hall Assembly was well integrated into the network of the Austin establishment, and Austin had been a relatively tightly knit community. However, the rift that arose between the Town Hall Assembly and.the Organization for a Better Austin divided the whole community. The resources were also split, efforts were often duplicated, and both the efforts and the resources were depleted as the groups battled each other.

11

Divergent Patterns of Change: An Interpretation

By now a picture has emerged of two communities facing racial change in different ways and with different outcomes. The differences were rooted in the nature of the communities at the outset, in the way the communities were dealt with by extralocal institutions, in the way they perceived themselves and were perceived by others, and in the way their residents, individually and collectively, sought to cope with changes they could not avert. All these conditions and circumstances were reflected in the way racial change unfolded.

The task remains to interpret these differences in some general way, attempting to draw out those aspects of the contrast that appear most significant. In what crucial respects did the two communities differ, and what general explanation can be given for Oak Park's apparent departure from the historical city pattern of total and rapid block-by-block racial turnover? By abstracting those most general aspects, perhaps we can look beyond the immediate cases toward issues relevant for other communities faced with change. While the findings of this study are not generalizable to the larger universe of cases, they do suggest important implications for social policy in this critical area of racial integration in housing.

Two distinctly different models could be applied. One, of course, is the ecological model that is most often used in analyses of racial change. The other is a model that focuses on normative dimensions of community as explanatory factors. Although neither model by itself can sufficiently explain the facts at hand, I believe that, taken alone, the second model is the more useful in the present case and that the ecological model, while relevant, falls short of predicting the pattern of racial change experienced in Oak Park.

Ecological Dimensions
of Racial Change

To assess the ecological model we must briefly recapitulate some of the community differences noted in the second and third chapters. The ecological perspective assumes competition for the scarce resources of housing and other facets of the residential environment. Thus the relevant factors are those pertaining to the ability of blacks and whites to compete. Housing cost and type and certain characteristics of the population may be considered key variables. The concept of community life cycle is also an important ingredient of the ecological model of transition.

Since black family incomes average roughly two-thirds those of whites in this country, housing cost obviously affects relative black-white demand in particular communities. It is true that median home values and rents were higher in Oak Park than in Austin. But if only the southern half of Oak Park—the area most immediately susceptible to racial change—is compared with Austin, the difference becomes much slighter.

It is possible that the cost of housing put a brake on black demand in Oak Park, but it does not seem a sufficient explanation for all the observed differences. It does not, for example, explain Oak Park's relative lack of concentration of the black population. Furthermore, while medians in Oak Park were higher than in Austin, there was substantial overlap in the range of costs of available housing.

Since the 1973 income-adjusted ratio of black to white home

ownership in Chicago was a low 0.38,[1] the proportion of renter-occupied units might be expected to influence black versus white demand for housing. The rate of renter occupancy is also sometimes considered important because it tends to imply a more mobile population. But Oak Park also had more rented than owned units, and its population was only slightly more residentially stable than Austin's.

In addition to the proportion of rental units, the size of the structure in which they are located is apt to be significant. Landlords living in a two-flat are probably more likely to resist renting to blacks than are absentee landlords of large apartment buildings. With this assumption we cannot expect a slow rate of transition in Oak Park, for units in large buildings were the modal type of apartment there. Some observers have suggested that the pattern of ghetto expansion in Chicago has been a fingerlike extension of black residence from ghetto areas along main traffic arteries, with subsequent filling up of the interstices. Oak Park had just such a likely thoroughfare in Washington Boulevard, which was also lined with large apartment buildings, and the outlines of such a pattern seemed to be developing there. However, most of those buildings were still continuing to draw white renters in 1977.

Nor do the population characteristics of Oak Park and pre-transition Austin support a conclusion that Austin was more likely to undergo rapid racial change. Both communities had a large number of elderly residents, for whom moving could entail severe hardship. If anything, the generally higher income status of Oak Parkers made them more able than Austinites to move when threatened with racial change. The influx of young white families that Oak Park experienced during the 1960s complicated the situation. If it is true that families with school-age children are among the first to leave changing neighborhoods, the pressure should have been toward faster transition. On the other hand, many of these families had come to Oak Park from changing neighborhoods in Chicago, and we do not know whether having moved once under such conditions makes people more or less likely to move again.

Both Austin and Oak Park had reached the end of a community life cycle, and both were therefore theoretically ready to be "passed down" to a lower status group for the cycle to begin anew. Again, the in-migration of the younger families in Oak Park adds a factor whose effect is difficult to assess. However, De Vise has argued that transition in Oak Park can be projected as a two-step process, with higher-status white Protestants first fleeing lower-status white Catholics and the latter group then fleeing the blacks.[2]

There is an inherent limitation in attempting to apply a strictly ecological analysis to this subject. One of the underlying assumptions of the ecological model is free competition. In fact, the absence of free competition in the dual housing market is most crucial.

For example, De Vise has calculated that the *potential* black population of Oak Park, assuming a color-blind housing market, is 14.3 percent, while Austin's is 24.0 percent. That is, if blacks were distributed throughout the metropolitan area in a pattern that was random except for their ability to pay for the housing, Oak Park would have a black population of 14.3 percent, and Austin one of 24 percent. This ten-point spread loses some of its apparent significance, however, when we take into account the proximity of the ghetto and the empirically color-conscious nature of the housing market. Oak Park's potential black population, according to De Vise's figures, is actually higher than that of two city community areas that were already 50 percent or more black in 1970. And of the six Chicago metropolitan municipalities with black populations of at least 50 percent, the black population potentials calculated by De Vise ranged only from 10.2 to 18.0 percent.[3] In other words, the black population potentials stand for the black percentages communities ought to have in an open market, not the maximum black percentages they might have in a dual market. I point this out because De Vise himself has suggested that certain communities are less likely to undergo transition because of low black population potentials, and I feel that this is a misinterpretation of the significance of such scores.

It can be construed, therefore, that Oak Park's potential black population, given the dual housing market in the Chicago metropolitan area, is far greater than 14.3 percent. The nature of the surrounding communities increases that potential, for the only likely directions for the ghetto to expand are north through Austin and west through Oak Park. The suburb of Cicero to the south has a metropolitanwide reputation for extreme violence toward any blacks who even venture across its border. Few Chicago-area blacks would be likely to risk moving there even in the unlikely event that they were able to secure housing. Other neighboring communities were also reputedly closed to blacks, though not so violently, and even Austin confined black in-migration to a rigidly contained block-by-block ghetto advance.

Introducing the concept of the dual housing market does help overcome the limitations of the ecological model and can help us understand what happened in Oak Park, if we are careful to distinguish between the rental market and the market for single-family homes. Oak Park's single-family home market was relatively open, but the rental market was much more racially discriminatory. Given the low tendency for black home ownership in the Chicago area, closing the rental market and opening the purchase market could allow some black in-migration while retarding the overall rate of transition. This seems to have happened to some extent in Oak Park. Nevertheless, the dual housing market model is not thoroughly applicable, either, since neither the rental nor the single-family home stock showed signs either of being retained as white preserves or of undergoing wholesale transfer into the black segment of the housing market.

But while Austin and Oak Park were socially and demographically similar, the similarity was far from perfect, and the ecological factors discussed here almost certainly must have had some effect on the patterns of change in Austin and Oak Park. Even so, attention to the ecological issues alone does not reflect or explain the nature of the differences observed. There were at least two clear signs that Oak Park was not undergoing racial succession of the classic type. One was the dispersal of black residence throughout the community. The other crucial indicator was that black occupancy of a housing unit did not preclude future white occupancy, for there continued to be white replacements for both white and black out-migrants. This was true even though Oak Park met most of the conditions that scholars have listed as conducive to racial transition: proximity to a large black residential concentration; aging and declining population; old housing stock; and preponderance of housing in rental units, to name a few.

In his review of the literature on ecological succession, Aldrich concluded that the ecological model still provides adequate explanation of cases of racial change and that, with few exceptions, attempts to intervene have been unsuccessful.[4] But at least one of the exceptional cases Aldrich cites—the Ludlow neighborhood of Shaker Heights, Ohio—was in a situation very similar to Oak Park's and employed some of the same intervention techniques later put to use in Oak Park. This leads us to suspect that the exceptional cases may not be freak occurrences, unrelated to one another and not amenable to general explanation. Rather, it suggests that we may fruitfully seek models that offer alternatives to classical ecology. In the remainder of this chapter, I offer such an alternative explanation.

Normative Dimensions

The discussion above suggests that normative dimensions of community may provide fruitful explanations and interpretations of the observations. The normative perspective combines both value and organizational dimensions. Therefore the relevant issues will be roughly separated into those pertaining to broad cultural values in the local community and those bearing on the community structure and decision-making network. Of course the latter also has its own particular value dimensions.

Values in the Local Community

Might Oak Park's directing its efforts toward integration rather than exclusion of blacks indicate an ethos that Banfield and Wilson have described as "public regarding"?[5] By this they mean the tendency—more characteristic of a middle-class, white Anglo-Protestant culture than of an ethnic culture—to organize for ends that are seen as for the good of the larger community and not necessarily in the group's immediate self-interest. We should expect Oak Park to have been more fertile ground for the growth of a public-regarding ethos than Austin, with its Irish Catholic tone and Irish-Italian population mix; and its reform-style government also fits the public-regarding paradigm.

But, given that grass-roots organization did not come into being in either Oak Park or Austin until a threat was sharply perceived, it seems that such organization was defensive in both cases and hence private- rather than public-regarding.

On the other hand, the presence of a viable and influential fair housing movement in Oak Park before most residents perceived a threat tends to support the thesis that a public-regarding ethos, which influenced community political goals, had been present to some degree. Once the community felt itself threatened, however, the fair housing ideology and rhetoric were no longer acceptable in their original form. The emphasis on simple nondiscrimination had to be replaced by an ideology and rhetoric that included terms such as "quota," "dispersal," "reverse steering," and so forth. Furthermore, the original fair housing organization was itself no longer viable. Yet the movement had had the important effect of defining Oak Park in the minds of residents as "open" and "integrated," however far from accurate that may have been. Therefore, in the later, racial-stabilization phase of activity, "maintaining the character of Oak Park" could be, and was, defined as maintaining an integrated community rather than a white one. This probably retarded panic by white residents. A few more blacks in an "integrated" community would not be as serious a threat as a few blacks who managed to crack the defenses of a "white" community.

A more important facet of political culture in Oak Park was its strong tradition of activism and volunteerism. Voluntary group activity had taken diverse directions and had the superficial appearance of extreme fragmentation. While Oak Park, with its

nonpartisan form and substance of government, was a conge-
nial home for amateur politicians, the bulk of civic activity was
directed toward a multitude of ends that were not strictly political. Such activity was turned into an ample reservoir of experience, example, and useful outside contacts when the stabilization effort began to take on its full proportions and when the
image-makers began to proclaim the "new Oak Park." The independent rallying of Oak Parkers to achieve such goals as
saving the financially impoverished and apparently doomed
botanical conservatory or the structural restoration and interior
refurbishing of Frank Lloyd Wright's Unity Temple became
prime features of the promotion aimed at selling the community. Needless to say, the "new Oak Park" and the ambitious
effort to sell it were direct outgrowths of the fear of massive
racial change.

Local boosters probably exaggerated Oak Park's volunteer
spirit. But the exaggeration had a self-fulfilling nature in that it
probably tended to draw to Oak Park new residents seeking
such involvement, and it may also have drawn old Oak Parkers
into the circle of activity. An impressive number of the more
energetic, enthusiastic, and prominent of the activists were
people who had lived in Oak Park a comparatively short time.
With a great boost from the metropolitan media, Oak Park was
able to get across the message that this was where good and
exciting things were happening. It became a viable residential
option for a type of young liberal who sought suburban
amenities yet tended to subscribe to the ideology that suburbs
in general were bland cultural wastelands of social irresponsi-
bility.

Those who sought community commitment found much opportunity for activity in Oak Park. Within the normal political
sphere there were many open hearings, and in Oak Park the
"open meetings" required by state law were construed as
forums in which discussion from the floor was always in order.
Village board and commission meetings sometimes lasted later
than 2:00 A.M., and adjournment at midnight was common.
That the same cast of characters circulated among these hearings seems less important than that an apparently satisfying
outlet was available to those seeking community involvement.

At least the illusion, and sometimes the reality, of citizen participation was a tenet of faith in Oak Park.

The values at issue here are both class- and community-linked. Oak Park represented an opportunity structure in which the value placed on civic participation, which tends to be associated with higher social status, could be freely expressed. Despite Austin's lively organizational life, political participation was made difficult by the relative absence of local channels of access to government. Incentives to participation were decreased because the avenues of influence were securely locked into the city political structure.

Of great importance—perhaps even essential—was the fact that Oak Park had an image that local leaders were able to strengthen and exploit. It was a suburb. More than that, it was a suburb with historic roots and an enduring cultural tradition. It was the center of the "prairie school" of architecture. Neighborhood preservation had a chance partly because Oak Park had a pronounced identity in the metropolitan area that easily lent itself to the belief that Oak Park was somehow especially worth preserving.

Yet this identity was not enough in itself to distinguish Oak Park from the onetime elite Chicago neighborhoods that, over the years, had declined into oblivion. Nor could Oak Park's brand of civic culture have had much influence by itself. Its sense of civic participation might have remained sterile. The important effect of all these symbolic aspects was to provide a cultural environment for certain patterns of structural arrangements, through which some of the ends related to maintaining racial stability could be accomplished. This pattern of organizational structure and process constitutes the critical difference in the efficacy of the responses to racial change in Austin and Oak Park.

Community Structure and Organization

No single term summarizes the important organizational distinctions between Oak Park and Austin better than "local community control." Leaders in Oak Park were able to take initiatives that led to some ultimate control over the rate and pattern of black in-migration and residential location; to influence those institutions whose policies and activities had real bearing on the process of racial change—for instance, schools, the real estate industry, and government agencies; and to forge a new identity for the community rather than having an undesired one thrust upon them.

The phrase "local community control" as used here is a broad rubric for a complex set of relations that cumulatively interacted to put in the hands of local elites the means of influencing the community's fate. The main structural features that in Oak Park added up to local control were autonomous government, the coincidence of the service areas of important government and nongovernment agencies and institutions, and the high degree of normative integration among individuals who were involved in activities that affected the course of racial change.

The obvious point about local government is that it has the resources of money and authority. In Oak Park it also had a high degree of moral legitimacy. Furthermore, it was willing and able to put its resources to work toward maintaining racial balance. It took few actions without assessing their effect on the racial situation, and virtually every branch and department of government could be used to further some aspect of the racial stabilization effort. Some of its initiatives were novel: for example, the application of the Delphi process to integration planning, the racial quota proposal, and the concept of home equity insurance.

It also engaged in comprehensive physical and economic planning, hired a professional public relations firm to handle publicity for the village, and passed and enforced a number of regulations cited earlier. Its Community Relations Department and its local fair housing law were respected as effective in-struments by fair housing leaders throughout the metropolitan area. As we have seen, it even moved the seat of village gov-ernment from downtown to a modern civic center in southeast Oak Park.

Austin had no local group or agency that could do things of such ambition and scope. The city government could have, of course, but Austin was just one of many communities competing for its share of the municipal resources. It also had to compete with other constituent groups whose interests were in some ways opposed to the interests the Austin community identified as its own—for instance, the real estate industry or the city's black community. "Preserving" Austin was not city hall's highest priority.

Community trust and support allowed Oak Park's local government to function informally as mediator in disputes involving other village groups and as central coordinator of the whole intervention strategy. The legal authority and official stature of local government were important in securing the cooperation of other community agents in actions that involved some measure of racial discrimination and could theoretically subject them to legal suit. It was important to landlords in the "counseling areas," to Housing Center leaders, and to real estate brokers to be able to point to the village government's explicit policy of "dispersal" as sanction for practices designed to retard black in-migration in east Oak Park. In their statements in interviews and in public meetings, real estate brokers seemed particularly concerned with the risk of violating federal and state fair housing laws. The Housing Center was quick to point out that its mode of operation was entirely in line with official village policy, even though the Housing Center had actually pioneered the tactics of "reverse steering" in Oak Park almost a year before the village's explicit statement on dispersal existed.

The second important structural feature was coincidence of service areas. When private or public agencies or institutions share common boundaries defining the territory or population they serve, we may say that their service areas coincide. When a large proportion of the important institutions of a local community share common boundaries, and when these also coincide with the perceived community boundaries, we may say that the community has a high degree of coincidence of service areas. This dimension of community has been identified by Roland Warren as one that creates meaningful distinctions among American communities.[6] The difference between Austin and Oak Park on this dimension was, in fact, of considerable consequence.

Some coincidence of service areas in Oak Park was a function of autonomous municipal government. But Oak Park's elementary school district was also coterminous with the village boundaries, and so was the township. This led to a convergence of interests that allowed the resources of such agencies to be solicited and applied toward the goal of achieving and maintaining racial integration. The school board, for instance, had its own reasons for being vitally interested in Oak Park's efforts to achieve a dispersed pattern of neighborhood integration, for resegregation of certain neighborhoods would mean de facto segregation of the schools. Therefore it moved early to raise the quality of the schools in southeast Oak Park. Still, it was ultimately forced to use busing to achieve racial balance, and in so doing it may have further contributed to the stability of the east Oak Park neighborhoods.

Members of the real estate board were also more likely to cooperate with the community's efforts to maintain integration, since Oak Park was their major market. Attempting to exclude blacks from the village was conceded to be futile, while steering whites away from Oak Park and marketing exclusively to blacks was hardly in the long-term interests of the local real estate brokers. Their best chance lay in hoping that the village's policy of dispersed integration succeeded and, therefore, in cooperating with that policy.

Austin, on the other hand, was fragmented by the crosscutting boundaries of important agencies and institutions. School attendance areas overlapped the community boundaries to serve neighboring communities as well as Austin. We may recall that redrawing the high school attendance-area boundaries in this way became a major community issue. Austin lay within five political wards, so that Austin residents did not have one common channel of access to government. Effective citizen pressure on the agencies that served the community was thus limited in some cases by the number of sources of the same service and in other cases by the responsibilities these agencies bore to communities other than Austin.

In short, attaining cooperation between local community elites and the institutions serving the community is easier when the needs and goals of the two are compatible, if not identical. This is more likely to happen when the same geographic constituencies are involved.

Our third factor, the high degree of normative integration in Oak Park's efforts to intervene in racial change, was partly a result of the role played by the village government, partly a result of the high coincidence of service areas, and partly a result of the intertwining of important organizations through the activities of individuals who held positions in more than one of them.

The significant consequences this structural feature had for the outcome of the racial stabilization campaign were that an extremely high level of diverse resources could be brought into play; and that it encouraged a sense of joint participation in a common effort with ultimate consensus on values and goals among the participant organizations.

A good illustration of the effect of this normative integration and consensus is the control Oak Park's leaders were able to exert over the housing market. This control was very much a function of the cooperation the village leaders had won from the real estate professionals. For instance, the much lesser territorial concentration of black residence in Oak Park as compared with Austin could not have been achieved unless the real estate professionals were willing to let blacks have housing in neighborhoods remote from the ghetto. On the other hand, whites continued to move into southeast Oak Park partly because they were not systematically steered away by the brokers and partly because they were steered to that area by the Housing Center and even by some real estate agents.

Therefore one key to the difference between Austin and Oak Park was the effective intervention by Oak Park leaders in the real estate market, altering the routine practices of brokers, lenders, and landlords; and one reason for the effectiveness of the intervention was that the relations between community groups, including the village government and the real estate industry, were never defined as overt and unmitigated conflicts of interests and goals, as happened in Austin.

An effect of maintaining tacit consensus in Oak Park was that contentions of issues, including the management of the real estate market, did not become defined as "zero-sum" games. The game in Austin had fixed rewards and clear winners and losers: if one group won a point, the opposition lost it.

In Oak Park, on the other hand, a definition of the situation was established that made concession possible without loss of face. In fact, concession was encouraged by the reward of good public relations, approval of peers, and acceptance as a bona fide member of the community in-group. A climate for cooperation was thus created, and the Oak Park community could not have exercised the control it did without the concurrence of the real estate industry. A concrete instance of that cooperation came when prohibition of "for sale" signs on property was ruled unconstitutional in 1977. Although the Oak Park ban on signs had been opposed by the Real Estate Board and, as I have described, almost led to a breakdown in the amicable relations between the realtors and the Community Relations Commission, the realtors decided in 1977 to continue their own ban on "for sale" signs on residential property, even though they were no longer legally compelled to do so.

Summary

Having now concluded the major part of our analysis, we must ask again: How useful is the comparison between Oak Park and Austin, and what do we learn from it? After all, we have seen that there were substantial differences between the two communities on a number of dimensions.

Yet those differences, whether of housing characteristics, social class, or history, did not lead the two communities' organizations to mount such very different responses to racial change. Strategically and tactically, what the organizations in the two communities tried to do was very similar. It is also worth noting that the responses in both communities reflected increasing levels of sophistication and organization in dealing with the relevant issues. Attention shifted from the small-time panic-peddler to the huge institutional complex of banks, mortgage brokers, FHA, and so forth. Groups became more concerned with subtle techniques of real estate steering than with blatant blockbusting. Competent leadership, wise to the workings of the real estate industry, existed in both communities. OBA, and also the larger Metropolitan Area Housing Alliance (MAHA) that, in a sense, OBA spawned, must be given a large share of the credit for bringing city- and statewide attention to the problem of financial disinvestment in urban neighborhoods. Gail Cincotta, certainly the most colorful of OBA's presidents and a founder of MAHA, was appointed by the governor of Illinois to a "blue-ribbon" panel to study the problem, and she later stood beside the governor on the dais as he signed the state's new antiredlining bill. Yet for all the skirmishes OBA won in Austin and the larger battles it won on a wider level, Austin could not achieve racial stabilization.

Oak Park surpassed Austin in effective local organization and the ability to define the situation on the local level; that is, among other things, to ward off the definition of Oak Park as a "changing" community. For reasons already described, there existed in Oak Park an encompassing organizational structure with both formal and informal dimensions, led by local community representatives. This structure included all or most of the key actors, rather than pitting some against others. The quantity and array of resources this put directly or indirectly under the control of local leadership was enormous.

Organizational integration coupled with local control was not the only difference between Oak Park and Austin; but it was the ingredient without which Oak Park's efforts to control racial change would very likely have ended as did Austin's. The effect and significance of its presence in Oak Park is clearer and more understandable against the backdrop of a case, such as Austin, where it is absent.

Despite the optimism of its leaders, Oak Park has not totally solved its racial problems. Black in-migration has been slow but is still accelerating. Even the most optimistic leaders acknowledged that Oak Park could not successfully integrate unless its neighboring communities could be persuaded or compelled to open their doors and unless blacks could be persuaded to seek homes there as well as in Oak Park. The dual housing market—both its institutional mechanisms and the perceptions of its existence by white and black home-seekers—has created a heavy burden that will not soon be overcome.

In the final chapter I will speculate on some of the factors that bear upon the future of Oak Park and some of the wider implications the Oak Park case may have for both urban theory and urban policy.

12

The Implications of the Oak Park Strategy

I have tried to probe the underlying reasons why Oak Park has succeeded so well in its racial integration strategies. Still, many questions remain. The one most frequently asked concerns that suburb's future. Is Oak Park likely to remain integrated, or will it follow the course of Austin and other communities in becoming all black?

Other frequent questions have to do with the implications of the Oak Park experience for race and housing in other metropolitan areas. Of what use, if any, is Oak Park as a model for urban or suburban housing integration? And if Oak Park were taken as a model, what would be the effect on black housing needs over the long run? Would the effect not be to restrict the housing supply for black people?

A final, even more general question has to do with whether a suburb differs significantly from a city neighborhood of comparable size and with comparable socioeconomic and demographic characteristics. Is there anything intrinsically "suburban" about suburbia? This last question is asked more frequently by scholars than by laymen, for the layman has a strong intuition that the answer is yes. For him, "suburban" is not just a subset of "urban." At least since the mid-sixties, however, sociologists have tended to answer that question no.

In this final chapter I will deal briefly with each of these issues. The questions do not evoke definitive answers, but I shall attempt to draw out some of the factors that we must surely take into account in even the most tentative of conclusions.

The Future of Oak Park

Oak Park still suffers many of the same liabilities, in its capacity to resist total racial turnover, as it did several years ago. At that time both experts and ordinary citizens commonly predicted that it would become predominantly black. It is still obviously on the edge of the ghetto, and black access to housing beyond the ghetto's fringe is still restricted, though perhaps not so severely as in the past. Black people can still move northward in Austin, as an alternative to settling in Oak Park, and they are in fact doing so, as Austin continues the racial transition that began more than ten years ago. However, there are some indications that this movement north may run head-on into an expanding Latino community on Chicago's northwest side. Farther east in the city, this largely Puerto Rican community has held the line against black residential expansion into its territory. If growth of the black community is shut off in this way, there should be increasing pressure on Oak Park's real estate market from black people in need of more and better housing.

In the meantime, Oak Park's housing stock and physical plant grows older, costs for maintenance and municipal service continue to increase, and economic development is described by many Oak Park leaders as the village's greatest problem, particularly as new shopping centers elsewhere compete for the local trade with Oak Park's mall and other commercial areas.

Then, too, Oak Park's black population continues to grow. While there is no justification for making predictions by simple linear extrapolation of this trend, neither is there any reason to predict a future leveling-off, giving Oak Park some stable, enduring black-white ratio. I have alluded earlier to "tipping points" and "self-fulfilling prophecies" of racial change. The two interact, and it is reasonable to say that a tipping point has been reached as soon as self-fulfilling prophecies take over—that is, as soon as large proportions of residents and outsiders begin to define the neighborhood as changing—regardless of the actual percentage or absolute number of the black population. By this formulation, the "tipping point" in Austin was very low, whereas it had not yet been reached in Oak Park in 1977.

But we must ask whether the relationship between tipping points and prophecies might not work the other way as well—whether there is a definite threshold, a certain proportion or number of black residents that virtually ensures that such prophecies will be made. This, in fact, is more consistent with the original concept of tipping point. Anthony Downs, for one, suggests there is.[1] Oak Park's advocates of a legal quota on black residency also apparently thought so. Actually, no one knows.

On the other hand, those who hope for stable integration in Oak Park can find grounds for optimism in the community's experience so far, particularly in that it has not conformed to traditional models of racial transition. The dual housing market has broken down there to the extent that blacks have not been transferred from white to black housing market segments, and units occupied by blacks may subsequently be occupied by whites, contrary to the definitive characteristics of the dual market paradigm. Oak Park has not been systematically red-lined, and though there has been real estate steering, it has not taken place on a scale sufficient to ensure transition in east Oak Park. Gradually, the negatively tinged definitions of Oak Park as "changing" appear to be losing their force outside the community. Thus leaders may hope that strategies that have apparently worked so far will continue to be effective, and that the conditions that have aided their success will continue to prevail.

Some of these conditions may actually be improving. The Oak Park housing market remains strong. A continued rise in home prices might retard black in-migration and would certainly retard in-migration by other than middle-class blacks. Obviously this is an improvement only from one point of view, but I am speaking here from the vantage point of Oak Park's leaders. Later I will deal with other perspectives and the troublesome legal and ethical issues involved.

Whether we are approaching some natural limit to suburban expansion is a point debated among urbanists. But, if some urbanists' predictions of a slowdown of growth on the metropolitan periphery hold, Oak Park, along with older inner-city neighborhoods, could benefit by even stronger housing demand.

Finally, the stepped-up pace of black suburbanization, together with widening of the cracks in the metropolitan housing market's dualistic structure, will help Oak Park achieve its aim of stability by expanding the range of housing choices for Chicago's blacks. To that end, the Oak Park Housing Center participates with nine other similar suburban placement services in a "fair housing network" that aided 155 black families in moving to predominantly white suburban neighborhoods in 1976.[2] While this is not a particularly impressive number, special censuses taken in selected Chicago suburbs since 1970 show that the total of such "nontraditional" moves by minority families is considerably higher.[3] Blacks may find it easier to move into the newer suburban communities than into the older established ones. The rapidly growing suburb of Bolingbrook, for example, had 27 minority residents in 1970 and 878 in 1975. The new community of Park Forest South increased its minority population from 54 to 1,520 between 1970 and 1976.

All these factors add up to little more than uncertainty about Oak Park's future; but, even so, its experience to date makes it exemplary among urban and suburban communities.

Oak Park as a Model for Neighborhood Racial Integration

Does the Oak Park example have meaning for other communities? Or is Oak Park really a very special case? In no sense is it a "typical suburban community"—if we can even assume such a thing exists. It is a middle-class suburb with a relatively affluent and well-educated population. Besides that, it has an architectual, historical, and cultural heritage that has immeasurably aided the local leaders' efforts at image-building. Even granting that Oak Park possesses some atypical advantages (but also some atypical disadvantages, such as the large proportion of rental housing units), could not some of the tactics employed there be advantageously transported to other communities?

While the answer to the last question is probably yes, few of the tactics put into practice in Oak Park were invented there. Most of them were borrowed from other communities' intervention campaigns. In its own method of combining and employing these tactics, Oak Park must be regarded as a model, but hardly as *the* model.

Few of the techniques actually were novel. One of these, the quota proposal, was scuttled. The concept of equity assurance was still being researched and developed in 1977, and it would be in operation in the next year. Use of the Delphi process in integration planning may represent a true advance in strategy, but it is still only a planning tool and means nothing without the wherewithall to execute the plan.

Management of integration in urban communities is properly described as a social movement, or at least as a part of the more encompassing fair housing movement. There are national and regional organizations, conferences, and newsletters to maintain formal and informal communication among leaders throughout the country. Within this framework, the ideology and technique of integration management are constantly evolving, so that any case—but especially an apparently successful case like Oak Park—presents a valuable contribution to practical knowledge.

Beyond that, however, Oak Park's major exemplary value may well be that it stands as an important negating exception to the rule that, in a dual housing market context, neighborhoods on the periphery of black ghettos will undergo transition, or that efforts to intervene in the process of ecological succession are normally futile. The definition of the situation is all-important, as we have seen. To control racial change, community leaders must be able to suppress definitions of the area as "changing." Those who wish to convince people that "it can be done" will be more credible if they can point to cases where it has been done.

The generally positive view of the Oak Park case taken here must be tempered by consideration of the ethical position and some of the potential consequences of an Oak Park type of strategy. To control racial change, Oak Park has resorted to tactics that may be unconstitutional. "Counseling," "reverse steering," "affirmative marketing" to whites, and "exempt location" are all practices that hinge on distinguishing between whites and blacks and are in that sense discriminatory. Whether or not they are constitutional, a matter on which no one seems entirely clear, there is still the issue of the practical effects of such tactics.

As long as a dual housing market exists, the primary way that additional housing units will become available to black people is by total transition of neighborhoods on the edge of the black ghetto. The more the movement of black people into these fringe areas is restricted, the lower is their supply of housing, the more limited their choices, and by simple supply and demand, the more they will end up paying for shelter.

Oak Park's strategy does result in such restriction and theoretically has those effects, although the practical significance of this case is limited by Oak Park's tiny share of the total metropolitan housing stock.

However, given the prevailing dual housing market and Oak Park's geographical location, completely open housing and stable racial integration are mutually exclusive goals. Ultimately the choice must be made for one of these ends over the other. Oak Park has value as a model that may contribute to lessening the kind of discrimination that results in total exclusion of blacks from white neighborhoods, while white people in fringe neighborhoods bear along with black people the cost of maintaining the dual market. In my estimation this overrides the immediate deleterious effect of the Oak Park strategy on black housing supply.

It should not be necessary to point out again that Oak Park's strategy is aimed at racial and not economic integration. The need to provide housing opportunities for low-income blacks outside city slums is altogether another matter. The panel of social scientists responsible for the National Academy of Sciences report, *Freedom of Choice in Housing*,[4] concluded that racial integration in housing was probably possible only so long as black and white residents were of the same social class. A majority of the black residents of the city of Chicago could afford to move into existing suburban housing;[5] but even if they did a large number of those who are financially incapable would still be left behind. The Kerner Commission identified as one of the country's major urban problems the confinement of blacks to central city ghettos, hemmed in by white exclusionist suburbs. But extending racial integration in existing suburban housing after the fashion of the Oak Park model not only would *not* be a solution to this problem, it would probably exacerbate it by drawing off more middle-class blacks from the city population, leaving proportionately even more of the hard-core poor in the central city. I maintain that the choice for a policy of racial integration must be made largely on the basis of values— ending racial discrimination as an inherently worthwhile goal—and not entirely according to the immediate pragmatic effects of policies to achieve racial integration. It is an unfortunate fact that many very worthy goals are not in the short run compatible with one another. Oak Parkers learned that setting priorities can be a painful process.

The City-Suburb Effect

The distinction between city and suburban community is important but not determinate. The characteristics of Oak Park's population and housing that differentiated it from Austin, particularly the social status of its residents and the cost of homes and apartments, were not necessary products of its suburban status, even though there is a very general empirical association of these attributes with suburbia. In many respects, however, Oak Park was not very "suburban" at all, as I have already pointed out.

We have seen, however, that suburban imagery and the legal territorial definition of the community had important roles to play in the construction of Oak Park's identity and its response to racial change. The presence of autonomous local government necessarily distinguishes the suburban municipality from the community within the metropolitan central city. Since many important services are municipally administered, this in itself should also lead to a higher degree of coincidence of service areas in the suburb than in the city community. However, it is not the fact of this distinction that matters, but its effect. The effect is to enable the local community to enlist the cooperation of government and other agencies and service bureaucracies and to co-opt their resources for local community-defined aims. In special circumstances this might be accomplished by a central city neighborhood—say when local leaders are particularly powerful within the city's larger political hierarchy. A case in point would be the Bridgeport neighborhood of Chicago's late mayor, Richard Daley.

Theoretically, the city-suburb distinction is also not directly relevant to the issue of normative consensus and integration, the third structural feature identified earlier as important to Oak Park's integration success. But the consensual style in Oak Park did not develop independently from its status as an autonomous suburb. For instance, note that Oak Park's reform government was inaugurated in 1953, just about the time when the class and ethnic barriers to residence in the suburb were being weakened. The switch to nonpartisan government helped keep the growing social cleavages from expressing themselves in local politics and helped reaffirm the old local establishment's control. Divisions did in fact emerge, and they were expressed in the growing Democratic vote in supralocal elections; but the split did not extend into the arena where local affairs were conducted and strictly local issues decided.

The effects of Oak Park's suburban status, then, were not necessary ones. Many suburbs are immobilized by internal conflict and fragmented by overlapping service districts. Suburbs that have developed their own local ghettos have often exhibited on a micro scale the same pattern of ghetto expansion as the central city and apparently have remained just as unable to counteract it. The argument made here is that the suburban effect is to increase the likelihood that a combination of ingredients will come together that encourage concerted community action directed at controlling racial change.

The real issue thus is not city-suburb, but the more general one of the degree of local community control and responsibility. The city-suburb distinction is just one of the ways differences among communities relative to this aspect can be expressed. Oak Park's leaders were, for reasons suggested above, more able than Austin's to control the means of the community's fate. They were also more responsive to the residents' interests as expressed through community and neighborhood associations. They were more susceptible to pressure from these quarters because they were not protected by large bureaucracies, political parties, distance from the citizenry, or much wider bases of support.

Ironically, one of the principal criticisms of proposals for reorganizing urban government to yield greater local community power has been that such a system would simply reinforce racial segregation. That has also been a common indictment of our suburban "patchwork" system of politically autonomous units. But the power to exclude blacks, as many suburbs including Oak Park have done in the past, is also potentially the power to integrate racially, as Oak Park's more recent experience has shown. Communities like Austin seem to have neither choice.

Notes

One

1 Ernest W. Burgess, "Residential Segregation in American Cities," *Annals of the American Academy of Political and Social Science* 140 (November 1928): 105–15.

2 Howard Aldrich, "Ecological Succession in Racially Changing Neighborhoods: A Review of the Literature," *Urban Affairs Quarterly* 10 (March 1975): 327–48.

3 Otis D. Duncan and Beverly Duncan, *The Negro Population of Chicago* (Chicago: University of Chicago Press, 1957).

4 Anthony Downs, "Alternative Futures for the American Ghetto," *Daedalus* 97, no. 4 (fall 1968): 1331–78.

5 Eleanor Wolf, "The Invasion-Succession Sequence as a Self-fulfilling Prophecy," *Journal of Social Issues* 13, no. 4 (1957): 7–20.

6 Chester L. Hunt, "Private Integrated Housing in a Medium Size Northern City," *Social Problems* 7 (winter 1959): 196–209.

7 Downs, "Alternative Futures."

8 Brian J. L. Berry, Carole A. Goodwin, Robert W. Lake, and Katherine B. Smith, "Attitudes toward Integration," in *The Changing Face of the Suburbs,* ed. Barry Schwartz (Chicago: University of Chicago Press, 1976); Marvin Bressler, "The Myers Case: An Instance of Successful Racial Invasion," *Social Problems* 8 (fall 1960): 126–42.

9 For example: Bressler, "Myers Case"; Berry et al., "Attitudes toward Integration"; L. K. Northwood and E. A. T. Barth, *Urban Desegregation: Negro Pioneers and Their White Neighbors* (Seattle: University of Washington Press, 1965).

10 Harvey Molotch, *Managed Integration* (Berkeley: University of California Press, 1972).

11 Morris Janowitz, *The Community Press in an Urban Setting*, 2d ed. (Chicago: University of Chicago Press, 1967).

12 Gerald D. Suttles, *The Social Construction of Communities* (Chicago: University of Chicago Press, 1972).

13 "Response to Racial Change in Austin" (unpublished manuscript, 1973). The research was conducted and the report prepared by Carol Corden, Carole Goodwin, and Katherine Smith under the direction of Brian J. L. Berry.

Two

1 Much of the historical information reported here is taken from Evelyn M. Kitagawa and Karl Taeuber, eds., *Local Community Fact Book, Chicago Metropolitan Area*, 1960 (Chicago: University of Chicago, 1963).

2 Ibid.

3 Raymond Hoover and Edgar Vernon, *Anatomy of the Metropolis* (New York: Anchor Books, 1962), p. 198.

Three

1 The VMA was the Village Manager Association, the main local political party, which had never been defeated. Although the south Oak Park precincts cast more votes against the VMA in 1973 than did other Oak Park precincts, south Oak Park still gave the VMA a comfortable majority.

2 The historical facts presented in this section can be found in a number of local histories. The major sources used were: Kitagawa and Taeuber, *Local Community Fact Book*, p. 198; Arthur Le Gacy, "Improvers and Preservers" (Ph.D. diss., University of Chicago, 1967); and Mrs. G. (F.) Hoagland, *Historical Survey of Oak Park, Illinois* (Oak Park: Oak Park Public Library, 1937).

3 *Oak Park Reporter*, 27 Feb. 1891, quoted in Le Gacy, "Improvers and Preservers," p. 65.

4 Betty Van Wyk, *Oak Leaves* (Oak Park), 12 June 1974.

5 Lois Wille, "Oak Park: The Hope of the Future," *Chicagoan*, December 1973, p. 60.

6 According to a professionally conducted "Architectural Survey of Oak Park," completed before the area was designated a national historical district.

7 Among others, Oak Park had Bramson's, Peck and Peck, and Marshall Field. Of these three, only the last remains.

8 Merlin L. Clark, *Religious Survey of Oak Park and River Forest* (Oak Park–River Forest Council of Churches, 1967).

9 "Oak Park Fact Sheet," a mimeograph distributed through the Oak Park Village Clerk's Office.

10 We rely on estimates released by the Oak Park Village Community Relations Department for data on black population since the 1970 census.

11 Research by Pierre de Vise, cited in Brian J. L. Berry and Frank Horton, *Geographic Perspectives on the Urban System* (Englewood Cliffs, N.J.: Prentice-Hall, 1970), pp. 413–19.

12 *Oak Park Comprehensive Plan* (Village of Oak Park, Ill., 1971), p. 24.

Four

1 A conservative estimate, based on the 1970 populations of the census tracts and gross observations of the extent to which they had changed, would give Austin a black population increase of no less than ten thousand during that period.

2 See, e.g., Aldrich, "Ecological Succession."

3 The best known of these studies is Luigi Laurenti, *Property Values and Race* (Berkeley: University of California Press, 1961).

4 Brian J. L. Berry, "Ghetto Expansion and Single Family Housing Prices: Chicago, 1968–1972," *Journal of Urban Economics* 3 (October 1976): 397–423.

5 Duncan and Duncan, *Negro Population of Chicago;* Molotch, *Managed Integration.*

6 The data were compiled by the Center for Urban Studies, University of Chicago, as part of a proj-

ect headed by Brian J. L. Berry. The primary sources were the lists of property transfers registered with the Cook County recorder of deeds published in *Chicagoland's Real Estate Advertiser*.

7 A thorough discussion of the dynamics of the dual housing market is contained in Molotch, *Managed Integration*.

Five

1 National Academy of Sciences–National Institute of Engineering, *Freedom of Choice in Housing*, Report of the Social Sciences Panel (Washington, D.C.: U.S. Government Printing Office, 1972), p. 27.

2 *Chicago Daily News*, 29 June 1972.

3 *Chicago Tribune*, 8 August 1971.

4 Rose Helper, *Racial Policies and Practices of Real Estate Brokers* (Minneapolis: University of Minnesota Press, 1969).

5 Records kept by the University of Chicago Center for Urban Studies of all property transfers for 1968–72 show that very few homes are transferred in older black neighborhoods. However, these records do not include contract sales of homes and therefore must underestimate the actual number.

6 Roberta L. Raymond, "The Challenge to Oak Park: A Suburban Community Faces Racial Change" (Master's thesis, Department of Sociology, Roosevelt University, 1972).

7 Helper, *Racial Policies*.

8 John Denne, address at Saint Catherine of Siena Church, Oak Park, Illinois, 19 April 1972.

9 See, e.g., National Academy of Sciences, *Freedom of Choice in Housing*.

Six

1 Downs, "Alternative Futures."

2 *Chicago Today*, 24 September 1972.

3 1970 census tract numbers 2518, 2519, 2521, 2522, and 2523.

4 See Paul E. Peterson, *School Politics, Chicago Style* (Chicago: University of Chicago Press, 1976), for more extensive discussion of the desegregation

plan and its fate within the larger context of Chicago school board politics.

5 Ibid.

6 Berry and Horton, *Geographic Perspectives*.

7 Ibid.

8 Molotch, *Managed Integration*, p. 183.

9 Ibid.

Seven

1 The theory underlying this discussion draws heavily upon Janowitz, *Community Press*, and Suttles, *Social Construction of Communities*.

2 Stanley Milgram, "The Experience of Living in Cities," *Science* 167 (March 1970): 1461–68.

3 Everett C. Hughes, "Dilemmas and Contradictions of Status," *American Journal of Sociology* 50 (March 1945): 353–59.

4 *Oak Leaves* (Oak Park, Ill.), 16 December 1970.

5 John Denne, Address at Saint Catherine of Siena Church, Oak Park, Illinois, 19 April 1972.

6 William Kornhauser, "Power and Participation in the Local Community," in *Perspectives on the American Community*, ed. Roland Warren (Chicago: Rand McNally, 1966), pp. 489–98.

7 Suttles, *Social Construction of Communities*, p. 51.

Eight

1 *Chicago Tribune*, 28 January 1973.

2 Franklin Dunlap, "Hi I'm Your Outraged Neighborhood Citizen on the March," *Chicago Tribune Magazine*, 5 December 1971, p. 48.

3 Ibid.

4 Ibid.

5 *Chicago Today*, 15 July 1970.

6 Ibid.

7 Dunlap, "Citizen."

8 Ibid.

9 Ibid.

10 Ibid.

11 Robert Bailey, *Radicals in Urban Politics* (Chicago: University of Chicago Press, 1972), is a book about the OBA that, among other things, discusses very well the inaccuracy of the public perception of the OBA as a radical group.

Nine   1 Oscar Newman, *Defensible Space* (New York: Collier Books, 1973).
2 *The World* (Oak Park, Ill.), 28 March 1976, p. 3.
3 For a description and analysis of the earlier fair housing effort in Oak Park, see Raymond, "Challenge to Oak Park."

Ten   1 *Oak Leaves* (Oak Park, Ill.), 15 July 1972, p. 16.
2 The term "horizontal" has been used by Roland Warren, *The Community in America*, 2d ed. (Chicago: Rand McNally, 1972), p. 13, to describe the "structural and functional relation of various local units to each other." This distinguishes these relations from "vertical" ones, meaning the relation of local units to extralocal units.
3 This is similar to a point made by James Q. Wilson, "The Strategy of Protest: Problems of Negro Civic Action," *Journal of Conflict Resolution* 5 (September 1961): 291–303.

Eleven   1 Council on Municipal Performance, "City Housing," *Municipal Performance Report* 1 (November 1973): 19.
2 Pierre de Vise, "The Annexation of Oak Park by Chicago" (Working Paper 8.16, Chicago Regional Hospital Study, December 1973).
3 Pierre de Vise, "Integration in the Suburbs— Who Needs It?" (Working paper 2.17, Chicago Regional Hospital Study, October 1973).
4 Aldrich," Ecological Succession."
5 Edward C. Banfield and James Q. Wilson, *City Politics* (New York: Vintage Books, 1963), pp. 38–43.
6 Warren, *Community in America*, p. 14.

Twelve   1 Downs, "Alternative Futures."
2 *Chicago Tribune*, 10 July 1977, p. 1.
3 Ibid.
4 National Academy of Sciences, *Freedom of Choice in Housing*.
5 De Vise, "Integration in the Suburbs."

Index